ROCK

YOUR

MIDLIFE

ROCK

7 STEPS TO TRANSFORM YOURSELF

YOUR

AND MAKE YOUR NEXT CHAPTER

MIDLIFE

YOUR BEST CHAPTER

ELLEN ALBERTSON, PHD, RD

Tiger Wellness Books
North Hero, VT 05474

Formatting by Lucy Holtsnider

Cover Design by Rebekka Mlinar

ISBN: 978-1-956592-01-6

For Marcia, my Mother, and Aly, my Daughter,
the two women who inspire me and helped me transform
into the woman I am today.

"People may call what happens at midlife 'a crisis,' but it's not. It's an unraveling—a time when you feel a desperate pull to live the life you want to live, not the one you're 'supposed' to live. The unraveling is a time when you are challenged by the universe to let go of who you think you are supposed to be and to embrace who you are."

— Brené Brown

TABLE OF CONTENTS

INTRODUCTION:

THE MIRACLE THAT IS MIDLIFE

There are two ways to live your life. One is as though nothing is a miracle. The other is as though everything is a miracle.

— Albert Einstein

Reaching midlife is a miracle. Until the 20th century, few people lived past fifty-five. If we leave infant mortality out of the equation, which accounted for 40-60 percent of the deaths of the total population, the average life expectancy between the 12th and 19th centuries was about fifty-five years. You finally got through menopause, kicked out the kids, and then you croaked!

Today the average life expectancy of women in the United States is eighty and a half years. Reach sixty-five, and there's a 46 percent chance that you will live to ninety.

Take a moment. Subtract your current age from ninety, and you've got a whole lot of living to do. How will you spend those decades?

At midlife, you're gifted with an entire second adulthood to know and love yourself on a deeper level. To figure out who you are and what you want. To take all the mistakes you made in your first adulthood, throw them in a makeover blender, and create a smoothie of an existence.

Blue-haired crone in a rocking chair, binge-watching *Jeopardy* and *The Golden Girls*? Forget about it! We want to rock midlife. As teens we listened to Aerosmith, Fleetwood Mac, and Cyndi Lauper; now we want to dream on, think about tomorrow, and have fun!

Nothing is written in stone, and anything and everything is possible. Change jobs (the average woman does it twelve times in her lifetime), partners, your hair color, your health, sell everything and move to a tiny house in a foreign nation, or travel cross country in an RV; it's up to you. You can transform who you are and how you live.

How do you start? Besides discovering the seven steps you need to transform and rock your midlife, which you will learn about in this book, you change your stories.

Begin by changing the story that you have no control over your life and that life is happening to you. That is incorrect. You are more powerful than you can possibly imagine, and life is happening for you. You are the heroine of your journey and the *author*-ity of your life. The old, outdated fables about who society, your partner, parents, kids, or peers said you should be can be rewritten into tales about who you want to be. The moldy "not _____ enough," unworthiness tapes can be erased and replaced by a new, positive self-concept recording.

As you'll discover in this book, you can literally change the structure of your brain by altering your thoughts and beliefs. This will create a cascade of different actions and habits, and a new *you* will start to emerge. By changing your stories and taking action, you can become the woman you've always wanted to be. By changing your thoughts you can manifest what you want in your life.

How do I know? Because that's what happened to me. I transformed my life and today can say I'm rocking my midlife by applying all that you'll learn about in this book. As a coach for midlife women (The Midlife Whisperer™), I've counseled and coached hundreds of women making the transition, and in this book, you'll hear their stories as well as my own.

Like a jungle tiger conditioned to live in a cage and jump through hoops for treats, we learn as children that we need to be a certain way in order to be loved and accepted.

To stay safe, we try to be perfect. When we're not, we judge and reject ourselves. We're told what's good and bad, and what's right and wrong. Starting right now, you can question what you were taught, change your beliefs about anything you'd like, and find a new truth.

Take Dandelions—growing up, they were the flower my dad loved to hate. To him, they were like pimples marring the perfect, velvety green lawn that he longed for. He'd curse the lemony blooms as he yanked them out with a fishtail weeder or his fists. Usually he'd only remove the top growth leaving the long, thick taproot to reproduce even more plants. He'd poison them with Roundup, plant grass to crowd them out, and decapitate them with the lawnmower. Like the bucked-toothed varmints in the arcade game Whac-A-Mole, no matter what Dad did to knock them down, they'd pop back up their smiling faces shining towards the sun.

As a kid I secretly loved the little flowers. I'd walk barefoot in the grass inhaling their musky scent. The little buds would get trapped between my first and second toes and dye my feet neon yellow. I'd weave them into my hair and pick bouquets for Mrs. B, my kindergarten teacher.

Stage four, the reproductive period when the yellow flowers transform into perfect snowy puffballs, was my favorite part of the dandelion life cycle. When Dad wasn't looking, I'd pick a perfectly round, white orb, make a wish, and blow.

The magical phase when the flower transforms is a wonderful metaphor for midlife. Like the mature dandelion, we can let our silver hair shine and allow our love and wisdom seeds to find fertile ground. We can make wishes and take action to make them come true.

Then I grew up, became a homeowner, and had a lawn of my own. Just like Dad, I'd curse those pesky dandelions. I'd pull them out with my own weeder, poison them, and cut off their heads with the push mower. Nothing worked. The dandelions didn't care or stop growing and proliferating.

When my children were toddlers, they'd dance on the dandelions with delight. As preschoolers, they'd make bouquets and weave them into their hair. Once my once tiny daughter, who's now twenty-four and bigger than me, picked a mature bloom and blew on it. "Aly, don't do that!" I screamed, grabbing her by the hand and redirecting her away from the lawn.

She didn't understand why I was so angry and hated these flowers. To her, they were beautiful playthings, more interesting than the green grass that I was coaxing to blanket the lawn.

She was right. Rather than labeling them an "obnoxious weed," I could have welcomed them into our yard.

Native to Eurasia, the plant was brought over from Europe in the 1600s. Named for the lion-toothed shape of their leaves (from *dent de lion*, French for "lion's tooth"), dandelions are beautiful, useful, and even nutritious. Dandy for your health, the plant is rich in vitamins, A, K, and C and is a good source of fiber, calcium, and potassium.

A member of the daisy family and one of the first plants to grow in the spring, they are an important source of food for bees, small birds, and butterflies.

The dandelion also creates a fertile environment for other plants. Their roots reduce soil compaction by creating air and moisture pockets underground. This aerates the soil, allowing other tender plant roots to grow and thrive. The long taproot also draws nutrients up into the topsoil, so other plants receive nourishment.

The yellow flowers resemble the sun and symbolize happiness, joy, power, and youthful energy. The white stage resembles the moon and symbolizes the dispersing of seeds and the power of wishes. No one stage is better than the other. Both the yin (sun phase) and yang (moon phase) are equally important.

Meditating on the humble plant's attributes can help you appreciate where you are in life, rise above life's midlife challenges, amplify hope, and attract good fortune, abundance, and prosperity. Blowing the seeds to the wind and making a wish will make you feel like a kid again.

Fifty years later, I've learned to love the Golden Poppy again. Today I live on ten acres of flat, fertile land that produces millions of dandelion seeds, so fighting or trying to control these flowers is futile. Along with the doves, robins, and red-winged blackbirds, we live in harmony with these ubiquitous weeds. Walking barefoot through the flowers, I feel peace where I once felt angst.

Throughout our lives, we learn to judge and label things. This flower is a rose and is good, this flower is a dandelion and is bad. Colored hair and smooth skin are beautiful. Wrinkles and gray hair are ugly and unacceptable. We are beautiful and productive at twenty-six and washed up and unattractive at fifty-six. Hustle culture and working until we're burnt out is good. Slowing down and savoring life is bad.

We start telling tales at a young age and continue to repeat these stories to define ourselves, determine the direction of our lives, and make sense of our experience. These stories, like skeins of wool, knit together communities, countries, and tribes, but they aren't always our own. They are passed down from parent to child or are imprinted media messages that we assume are true. Not only do these narratives transmit information, they also confer and confirm our identity, and may even serve as a moral compass.

My labeling and judging of the dandelion had created a story that obscured a deeper understanding of the flower's life. Today, I see how our lives can be like the lifecycle of the dandelion. We start out as a seedling and germinate. In our formative years we are new plants, tiny rosettes tenderly exploring who we are and how we fit in.

To stay grounded and hydrated, we grow deep roots. Faced with change and challenges, our leaves morph from smooth to jagged. Al dente like, we become toothsome, hardier, like the mature dandelion plant.

In the early spring of our lives, we flower. Like the dandelion we grow multiple buds, reproducing ourselves to fit into various roles: daughter, sister, mother, friend, wife, neighbor, worker, boss. When the sun shines, we open to the light. Everything seems possible, and we expand and grow taller. When it's dark, cloudy, or the weather conditions of our lives are poor, we close up until the storm passes and the light returns.

When budding is done, like a caterpillar spinning a cocoon, the dandelion flower shuts so seeds can grow. We too morph, closing up and questioning who we are as we go through menopause and empty nest, perhaps experience divorce or lose loved ones and grieve. This refines and redefines us.

Once that transition passes, we are no longer the youthful yellow flower, but damn, we can still be productive! We open up, let our hair shine like the dandelion puff in its final crescendo stage. We lighten up, make wishes, and love ourselves enough to work on our dreams and have the faith that they will come true.

We can remember the tender youthful times with fondness, but now we're different: wiser, more powerful, and able to know ourselves in a deeper way.

Letting go of the insane, culturally-driven compulsion to look the way we did in our twenties and thirties, we can embrace how beautiful we are today. Rather than berating ourselves because our bodies have changed and don't measure up to the impossible beauty standards designed to make us hate ourselves so we'll buy products and services to fix our perceived flaws, we can appreciate function over form.

Like the dandelion we can be prodigious, producing copious seeds that impact neighbors and blow nourishment out into the world. No one can control us or tell us to stop spreading our truth. We can question stories about dandelions and ourselves. Like the war on dandelions, the war with ourselves is one we cannot win. Like the dandelions, midlife women are here to stay. It's time for us to take up more space. Life's too short to beat ourselves up and get bent out of shape by what society tells us is our truth.

This book is your invitation to transform yourself and be like the dandelion in its mature magnificence. In three parts, I will inspire, guide, and help you to jumpstart a new life, a next chapter that is your best chapter. It is my sincere wish that you step into this exciting stage of your growth and development, embrace it fully with heart and mind, and using the tools, advice, and activities I offer as support, learn to rock your midlife.

Rumi, the 13th-century Persian poet, gives you a peek preview of the journey ahead:

> *Out beyond ideas of wrongdoing and rightdoing, there*
> *is a field. I'll meet you there.*
> *When the soul lies down in that grass, the world is*
> *too full to talk about. Ideas, language, even the phrase*
> *"each other" doesn't make any sense.*

PART I

MIDLIFE MADNESS

1

THE WRONG SIDE OF FORTY

*Maybe the journey isn't so much about becoming
anything. Maybe it's about un-becoming everything
that isn't really you, so you can be who you were
meant to be in the first place.*

— Paulo Coelho

Forty hit me hard. I had absolutely no idea what the %$^# to do with my life. My thirties were a roller coaster ride, a delirious éclair filled with fame and fortune, and frosted with foie gras. My then husband and I were literally The Cooking Couple— the king and queen of food and romance for the PG audience, and scientifically proven aphrodisiacs and sex for the R-rated crowd.

The ride started when our bestseller, *Food as Foreplay: Recipes for Romance, Love, and Lust*, hit the stands on Valentine's Day. Sandwiched between pages 85 and 86, the centerfold showing us in bed with champagne, chocolate, and a ginormous lobster, was everywhere—*Glamour, Playboy, USA Today, EXTRA . . .*

Doors opened. We landed a nationally syndicated radio show, lucrative endorsement gigs, television appearances, and a six-figure contract with Simon and Schuster for a second book called *Temptations.*

Then Viagra and 9-11 happened. People were scared and confused. They weren't buying books and didn't need aphrodisiacs. *Temptations* tanked. Plus, Kim Cattrall, aka Samantha Jones from *Sex and the City,* came out with a competing book, *Satisfaction: The Art of the Female Orgasm* that Valentine's Day and sucked up all the prime television slots with her take on how to slide frictionless between the sheets.

Frankly, my soon-to-be ex and I were sick of the act and working together. Talking about the merits of chocolate, donuts, and licorice (a turn-on for men according to the Chicago Taste and Smell Treatment and Research Center) and basil (used in Voodoo love ceremonies in Haiti) was getting stale. We joked about writing books in our golden years about gumming down oysters chased with a ginseng/ginkgo shot. So we quit being The Cooking Couple, which was a source of tremendous tension in our relationship. While we had great chemistry on-air, beneath the laughter and chocolate-smeared lingerie simmered negativity, resentment, and anger that wasn't resolved until I finally couldn't take it anymore, and left.

Life moved on. There were two kids to care for and a next chapter to figure out. I prayed for direction. A few days after officially ending The Cooking Couple, I received a postcard from the National Center for Strength and Conditioning, inviting me to become a certified personal fitness trainer. I'd always been a jock, and the training was worth seventy-five continuing education units that I needed to maintain my status as a registered dietitian, so I signed on.

I loved being a trainer, but it was a dangerous profession for me. Addicted to exercise and suffering from negative body image, the job was like being an alcoholic working in a liquor store. I worked out with all of my clients—four to six hours a day—*and* led group exercise classes! But no matter how much I exercised and how little I ate, my body fell short of the perfection I was seeking.

Perfectionism is a theme that's haunted me for decades. I wanted everything—my body, marriage, children, career, credentials, and house to be perfect, whatever that means. It's a common happiness hurdle for many women I know and work with at midlife, especially those of us born between '62 and '69 when Uranus was in Virgo, an astrological sign characterized by perfectionism. The trait makes life feel like an endless report card that can strangle the joy from existence.

I look at the bicep-popping, stomach-ripped pictures of myself during that time with the rock-hard glutes and a phony, happy face, knowing hours earlier I had popped an antidepressant, and I wonder, Who was I? Why was I so miserable? What caused me to drive myself to the point of exhaustion day after day?

As I handed my size 4, high-end clients dumbbells and listened to them complain about their muffin tops and flabby arms, bedrooms needing redecorating, and miserable marriages *again,* I thought: There's got to be more to life than getting up at 5:00 a.m., ripping my body to shreds, and returning to a home where I work more (I was completing a doctorate) and feel unloved and unappreciated. Am I going to keep going like this year after year until I'm completely burnt out? I'm exhausted, depressed, and my mind is turning to mush. Where did the brilliant, creative woman who wrote books and spoke to thousands go? What happened to the hippy chick who belly danced along the Charles River, read Tarot cards, and practiced Reiki? I just want to wake up energized (sans Starbucks), joyful, and excited to start my day!

And then Cynthia died. She was an amazing woman and a wonderful friend.

Beautiful, blonde, vivacious, the life of the party, she'd greet you at the door with a hug and a drink. Once she fixed me something called The Bee's Knees. The boozy brew made from gin, lemon juice, and honey left me buzzing. She knew it would be strong, but that was Cynthia: Bold, full-bodied, always challenging her friends to live large and on the edge.

Cynthia was three weeks older than me, the first friend my age to leave the planet.

One day she was laughing and enjoying life, and the next, just days before her 53rd birthday, she sent me a Facebook message: "I have cancer. Liver, bowel, maybe lung. Just found out last night."

Cynthia's death was a wake-up call that made me feel deeply grateful for my life, mindful of my mortality, and aware that I needed to transform my life because I was running out of time. I craved self-love and acceptance. I needed to figure out how to be authentic, follow my heart, and make something amazing happen that generated joy and vivacity. Just how I did this is captured in stories you'll read throughout this book.

YOU, TOO?

I'm assuming you picked up this book because you're dissatisfied and yearning for change. Maybe your life looks great on the outside—like a perfect, shiny apple—but your soul is rotting within, and you want to find your passion and purpose.

You "thought" you had everything you needed to be happy: the house, hubby, kids, career, but you can't remember the last time you laughed or experienced an iota of joy. Perhaps you feel stuck, dissatisfied, trapped, and don't have the courage and confidence to do what scares you. You want to do things that are unconventional, adventurous, and exciting, but it feels unrealistic, an impossible mission given the current confines of providing consistency and stability for yourself and your family. Exhaustion (because you've ignored your needs for too long while taking care of everyone else!) is making it difficult to even contemplate change. And those ANTs (automatic negative thoughts) are hijacking your peace and making it difficult to discover what's truly important for you, so you can change your trajectory and be happy.

I hear you, and I gotcha. I may have more degrees than a thermometer, but I'm proudest of my proven track record as a coach helping hundreds of women, including myself, transform their lives. I am going to share the secrets you need to rock your midlife and make your next chapter your best chapter. In the pages ahead, you'll learn how to change the old internal tapes—the thoughts, habits, and beliefs that are keeping you stuck—and shift your energetic vibration so you feel (and look!) great, and attract what you truly want. You'll heal physically, emotionally, spiritually, and finally feel motivated, inspired, authentic, and empowered.

That longing so many women in their forties and fifties feel for a metamorphosis isn't a midlife crisis. That desire is your wake-up call. We've been gifted with a second adulthood. How would you like to spend it? Write a book or start a business? Find or reignite romance? Create a beautiful, healthy body? Travel? Follow your calling, your bliss? Find meaning, purpose, and peace, so in twenty-five to thirty years, you'll have no regrets and look back and go, Wow!

All you have to do to start is say yes to yourself and your life and set an intention to change. Okay, you may piss some people off, and you will definitely have to face your fears and do what scares you, but trust me, it will be worth it.

The midlife scenario we know too well—crisis, catastrophe, hot mess—is total BS. Yet the misconception remains. Put "midlife" in Roget's Thesaurus and "middle age" and "the wrong side of forty" are the only synonyms that appear. Google "midlife" and it's conjoined with its parasitic twin "crisis" as a distressing time associated with plastic surgery, buying a sports car, or having an affair.

The cliché glosses over the inner turmoil many women experience. That angst is your starving soul screaming to be fed so it can grow, and getting a tummy tuck or Porsche isn't going to catalyze the transformation you're craving.

As researcher, author, storyteller, and mid-lifer Brené Brown writes in her blog, "To call what happens at midlife 'a crisis' is bullshit. A crisis is an intense, short-lived, acute, easily identifiable, and defining event that can be controlled and managed. Midlife is not a crisis. Midlife is an unraveling."

SO WHAT IS MIDLIFE, ANYWAY?

I'm here to validate your struggle and encourage you not to ignore the voices in your head and the cauldron of smoldering, gray emotions that are driving you bonkers, keeping you up at night, and making you miserable. Pay attention to what is happening inside—the anxiety, depression, frustration, and confusion you're feeling are all there to help you admit that everything's not okay, even if from the outside your life—the 2.5 kids, dog, and house in the suburbs—looks like what you thought adulthood should be.

Complex changes occur at midlife. The period of metamorphosis is ripe for new beginnings and endings. Children leave home, and aging parents need attention. Illnesses and health challenges surface. Careers and work that once fit perfectly suddenly feel unfulfilling. The strong marriage you took for granted is on the rocks, and either you need to fix it, or like I did, file for divorce.

The changes aren't just occurring on the outside. Like a caterpillar turning into a butterfly (actually totally digesting itself by excreting enzymes that dissolve all its tissues except for a few imaginal cells) you're morphing from within. A cascade of internal hormonal fluctuations impacts body and mind. Brain fog replaces mommy brain. While our daughters face the "freshman 15," often gaining that extra weight in their first year of college, we battle the "menopausal 10." Anxiety, moodiness, and insomnia increase, and libido decreases. It feels like you're riding a merry-go-round, but instead of horses, you're sitting on shifting levels of estrogen, progesterone, and testosterone, leaving you stressed, harried, and anxious as though your world is falling apart.

This low is normal and natural. As journalist Jonathan Rauch points out in his book, *The Happiness Curve: Why Life Gets Better After 50,* a large body of research shows that there is a U-shaped curve in self-reported life satisfaction scores that cuts across the human race. Most, if not all of us hit a low point at midlife. As Rauch explains, "it's not just a crisis" but "a change in our values and sources of satisfaction, a change in who we are." He calls it the dawn of "encore adulthood" and defines it as a new stage of adult development that is reshaping how we think about retirement, education, and human potential.

WAKE UP CALL FROM THE UNIVERSE

The internal and external changes at midlife are a spiritual wake-up call from the universe. As the ground beneath you breaks along your fault lines, there's a release of energy causing a seismic shift and creating an opportunity to enter a new stage of being, to start fresh, reinvent, tap into your inner light, and grow and glow.

What's the downside of this new dawning? It's disconcerting and terrifying. Like a colt taking its first wobbly steps or a sparrow jumping out of the nest for the first time, you feel scared, doubtful, and uncertain. The old strategies you've used to navigate your life and feel better no longer work. That unsettled feeling forces you to ask tough, probing questions about your identity, such as: Who exactly am I? Where do I fit in? What do I want to do with the rest of my life?

At midlife, the cozy, comfortable nest egg you built starts to crack. Internally, you feel claustrophobic, confused, and restless and long for space, meaning, and purpose. There's a desire to evolve from the inside out into something fresh, substantial, and new, which sets the stage for shell shock. Change occurs in the external world to crack your heart open, so you can rebirth, rebuild, reinvent, and finally love yourself.

Here's some good news. This isn't your mother's mournful midlife. Rest and retire? Forget about it! Midlife is a fresh beginning, or it can be if you harness change to create a new life you love.

Forty years ago when my brother left for college, my mom felt her reason for being (i.e., motherhood) was ending. All she could do was mourn. She'd go down to my brother's room, play his records, and cry. In contrast, when my daughter left for college, I was sad and emotional, but I also felt celebratory. Both of us were starting exciting new adventures. I had more space and time to feed my urges and desires—to make a difference in the world, take care of myself, follow my passions, and work on my own goals and dreams.

Trust me, while change feels crazy and uncomfortable, it's exactly what you need to become who you're supposed to be and begin the work you're meant to do in the world. When you face the fears ignited by change, you build self-confidence and can leverage this power to write your next glorious chapter. You have everything you need to succeed. The blueprint to transform is already inside of you. You just need the keys to your new castle, which I'll provide in this book.

As you'll discover when you follow the seven steps in the pages ahead, your midlife adventure starts with knowing and loving yourself on a deeper level (Steps 1 and 2). Then in Step 3, you'll learn how to go from pooped to supercharged so you have the energy and vitality (and maybe a few fewer pounds) to take advantage of the thirty-year bonus that today's medical breakthroughs make possible. Next, in Step 4, you'll discover how to reprogram your brain so you can be happier, clearer, and more creative. In Step 5 of your midlife journey, you'll become empowered and learn how to go from helpless to in charge. Once you're strong and confident, you'll be ready for Step 6, taking on rehabbing your relationships. You'll need this because people in your life may no longer recognize the new, awesome you! In this step, I'll also share proven techniques to improve your communications with friends, lovers, family members, and co-workers, so you can get the love and support you deserve. In the final step, Step 7 you'll learn how to tap into the enlightened life, moving from bottomed out emotionally to lifted up spiritually.

And, of course, I'll be with you every step of the way, holding your hand and providing resources to help you transform yourself and make your next chapter your best chapter. In Part III: Putting It All Together, I'll provide a 7-day Action Plan so you can jumpstart your next chapter over a period of one week, taking all that you've learned to get started in bite-sized portions.

Life transformation is like an operation. When you're in the O.R., there's no such thing as minor surgery. Yes, change is turbulent and emotional, but if you listen to your heart, you'll move through the seven steps in the right direction and build a fulfilling second act. There's a world filled with sweet possibilities waiting for you. May you create a life that is more fun and fulfilling than you ever imagined, and wake up joyful, energized, and excited every day.

Download your free *Rock Your Midlife Playbook*[1] to support you, then turn the page and let's get started.

2

GETTING UNSTUCK AND BIRTHING
SOMETHING NEW

My own brain is to me the most unaccountable of
machinery – always buzzing, humming, soaring,
roaring, diving, and then buried in mud. And why?
What's this passion for?

— Virginia Woolf

Claire was stuck. It was life in the time of Covid, and all her plans to travel, relocate, and swap teaching for a coaching career had come to an anticlimactic halt. Add a heaping dose of grief from losing both parents, the discomfort of gaining twenty pounds, and selling her condo at the wrong time, and Claire was immobile. Shut down by shame, she felt like a failure before even starting her next chapter. Getting up in the morning and taking a shower were all she had energy for. Her cholesterol had jumped one hundred points in two years, and her health was suffering. Hot and uncomfortable, Claire felt like she was wearing a heavy bearskin coat. Unless she made a conscious effort and took action, the state could persist for years.

"I feel so sorry for myself because I'm completely on my own," she told me at our initial session. "I feel shattered and want to feel settled and have a purpose."

As we talked, I pulled a Tarot card from the deck on my desk, which I do for all of my coaching sessions. This reveals the B-side— the underlying or subconscious issues and energy that even the client may not be aware of. Out jumped the Eight of Swords, the perfect card for the muddy state of mind keeping Claire stuck.

Feeling immobile at midlife, as Claire was, looks like the Eight of Swords. The card pictures a woman who is bound and blindfolded. Surrounded by eight upright swords, she looks trapped—stuck in the mud and unable to move. Behind her is a castle representing everything she wants—the hopes, desires, and dreams that feel unattainable. She's unable to get what she wants because she's frozen by her circumstances and imprisoned by her limiting beliefs represented by the swords, the suit which symbolizes the mind.

THE MIDLIFE TRAP

Whether the circumstances are a difficult relationship, an unfulfilling job, or massive debt, like the figure in the Eight of Swords, many women are out of alignment at midlife and lose their way. Why? First, we're flat out exhausted, which is why Step 3 in the book, which is about staying energized, is so important. Second, we're so busy pleasing and taking care of others that we've lost connection with ourselves. Having surrendered our power to someone or something outside of our self we feel like a victim—hopeless and alone.

Growing up watching Disney princesses like Snow White and Sleeping Beauty (Where were Mulan, Anna, Elsa, Moana, Raya, and Merida when we needed them?) who find redemption in a prince, we long for someone to rescue us. Ironically, what we need to do is rescue ourselves by taking back our power and personal responsibility. We do this by first removing the blindfold, so we can see that we do have options.

Even if we don't like the options, knowing that we have choices is empowering. Once we accept where we're at and decide to move forward, we can remove the ropes that bind us, step out of the mud, walk away from the sword mind trap, and hike to higher ground.

Feeling stuck, along with weight gain and low confidence is one of the biggest hurdles women at midlife face. It's about as easy to avoid as wrinkles, gray hair, and menopause, except there's no Botox, Nice 'N Easy, or HRT to make it disappear. That's because at midlife, we're often so deeply dug into our current reality that we don't see a way out. The only women I see who don't feel stuck are the courageous souls who followed their hearts earlier in life and created a life in alignment with who they truly are.

Should I stay stuck or go? is a hard question because we're "comfortably uncomfortable"—conditioned to repeat the circumstances of our lives day after day, even though they leave us feeling desperate and depressed. The pursuit of happiness may be an inalienable right, but the human brain is designed to keep us safe so we can survive and reproduce. Don't worry though, I'll provide efficacious tools to jump over this happiness hurdle.

You may be in a long-term marriage that no longer works but offers security and definition, have a job you hate that provides a steady paycheck, or be faced with a health issue that feels too overwhelming to address. So you stay stuck for years or even decades. That's a shame because all you have to do initially is wiggle out of the ropes and take off the blindfold so you can see things more clearly. Once you do that, you can take that first step toward higher ground where your castle is.

When I ask women at midlife what their biggest challenge is, it appears over and over again as some version of what Hillary told me:

"I'm feeling stuck. I started a project recording my own music four years ago and walked away due to fear, overwhelm, and a lifetime of unacknowledged feelings and emotions. I'm now forty-one years old."

Or Lynn: "I feel stuck, trapped in my current responsibilities and life structure. I have fleeting moments of excitement about doing something that feeds my soul, but can't seem to get to that place."

Or Nan: "I am challenged, not in a good or productive way, by my job and feeling unsatisfied and stuck."

Or Meredith: "I am totally stuck. I can't seem to determine where to focus to find happiness in my life."

Being stuck at midlife feels like mud season, the approximately six-week period in late winter and early spring that New Englanders love and hate. We love it because it means the snow is melting and spring is here. We hate it because dirt roads become a gooey mess, making driving a pain in the axle. If you drive on a muddy road, your tires can easily get stuck.

While it's possible to avoid mucky roads entirely by taking another route, once you are stuck you have to employ strategies to get free or you risk the danger of abandoning the vehicle of your life to depression, resentment, or desperation all of which, as you'll learn in Step 5: Empower Yourself, are not vibes that will catapult you forward.

Fortunately, like the woman in the Eight of Swords Tarot card, getting unstuck and out of the muck only requires one thing to start: shift your mindset. This is a foundational move you'll need to successfully apply my guidance in Part II's 7 Steps. Shifting your mindset may seem like a big project, but you can get started by enacting four things: 1) stop ruminating, 2) quit procrastinating, 3) overcome your "immunity to change," and 4) face your fears.

MINDSHIFT #1: RUMINATION:
THE MUCK THAT KEEPS YOU STUCK

Rumination, chewing thoughts over and over in your mind the way cows and other ruminants chew their cud, is one of the leading reasons women stay stuck at midlife. While it can feel like a productive strategy because your brain is actually doing something, ruminating is like gunning the engine when your tires are stuck in the mud. The harder you press down on the accelerator, the deeper your tires sink and the less traction you have.

Rather than ruminating, you need to stop the woe-is-me storyline and playing the role of victim. Once your mind stops spinning, you can analyze the thoughts and beliefs that keep you stuck. Then you can become solution, rather than problem, focused. Solutions are like the piece of cardboard you place under your car tire to give you traction to escape the mud. The universe will steer you, but you have to stop spinning long enough to drive slowly forward until you reach solid ground.

The first move is to stop being trapped by your thoughts. This is difficult because humans naturally ruminate. Like a Guernsey munching grass, we masticate. This is our brain's natural response to problematic situations. While rumination feels like taking action, it sinks you further into the mud. According to Yale professor and psychologist Susan Nolen-Hoeksema, author of *Women Who Think Too Much*, there is evidence that "Rumination exacerbates depression, enhances negative thinking, impairs problem-solving, interferes with instrumental behavior, and erodes social support." In addition, rumination (aka being a worrywart) is linked to depression and anxiety, making it even harder to escape situations that are no longer good for you.

From a Law of Attraction perspective, which you'll learn more about in Step 5, rumination is deadly. According to the Law of Attraction, like attracts like. Thoughts are energetic, and emotions are magnetic. This means that if you think positive thoughts and generate positive emotions, that energy attracts positive outcomes. Conversely, if you worry and feel blue all the time you continue to attract problematic energy and only see troubling outcomes. In other words, you get what you think and feel.

Focusing on positive emotions isn't just woo. As you'll learn in Step 4: Reprogramming Your Brain, research from psychologist Barbara Fredrickson suggests that positive emotions broaden our awareness and ability to act, which builds personal resources.

It's okay if you can't see a clear way ahead. Our minds often can't conceive of what's next because we've never experienced it before. You can't see the big picture yet because your problems feel huge and daunting, so that's all you see.

No matter how stuck you feel, you can shine a light on your staled state by noticing when you are ruminating. Starting a meditation practice can help because it teaches you how to observe rather than be taken over by your thoughts. Sitting quietly and observing your mind can help you see that thoughts are things. They can be positive, negative, or neutral. Whatever their flavor, you can decide which thoughts to follow and which to let go of. Meditation can enable you to put your mind in its proper place as the servant, not the master.

You'll start to sort mind swords into solvable versus "gravity" problems. The concept of gravity problems comes from two engineers, Bill Burnett and Dave Evans, authors of *Designing Your Life*. Like gravity, these problems are fixed: you can't fight them or take action to fix them. The only way through is acceptance.

For example, you may have an inherited health problem, a horrible boss, or a spouse who won't change. When you understand the thing that's keeping you stuck is a gravity problem, you can stop dwelling on it because it defies change. Rather than getting stuck on a problem that you can't change, Burnett and Evans offer two choices: reframe the situation as an opportunity to learn and grow or walk away.

It's very helpful to remember the serenity prayer here:

God grant me the serenity
to accept the things I cannot change;
courage to change the things I can;
and wisdom to know the difference.

Once you accept a difficult situation, even if it's a gravity problem, you can then take responsibility for your own happiness. This mind shift alone will have you sailing out of the mud. You'll feel freer, and that energy will enable you to slowly head towards the infinite number of possibilities that are available to you.

MINDSHIFT #2: PROCRASTINATION

I should be writing; my deadline for the first draft of this book is due in ninety-six days, but I'm procrastinating. In the last 15 minutes, I've… gone upstairs twice, to go to the bathroom, to get water, make tea, and talk with Ken, my fiancée. I've done two sets of pushups, *and* checked my Instagram feed three times. I'm putting off getting my butt in the chair and starting. Why?

Procrastination: We all know it. We all hate it. Whether over taxes, dating, starting a fitness program, updating that resume, or cleaning the house, we all do it. Even when you get unstuck, procrastination can cast a shadow over your life, so you can't seem to get the things you want to do done.

The word procrastination comes from the Latin *procrastinare,* which means "to put off till tomorrow."

"Procrastination is one of the most common and deadliest of diseases, and its toll on success and happiness is heavy."

—Wayne Dyer

If it's so painful, why do we engage in the unproductive behavior again and again, until it becomes habitual? Why do we put things off? Why don't we just do what we need to do when we need to do it?

There are a couple of reasons. First, procrastination is the rope in a game of tug-of-war between your future and present self. It's the look great in your skinny-jeans next-month versus eat the donut now. Your future self wants to look fabulous in your Levi's. Your present self wants instant gratification, that sugar rush triggered by the honey-glazed cruller. Since you live in the present, unless you employ psychological tricks, your present self usually wins especially if you're hungry and stop at Dunkin's for coffee or the break room where your co-worker has conveniently left a baker's dozen.

Procrastination is actually trying to help you. She means well and wants to keep you safe. Sure we want to do new things, but part of us (the ruminator) is worried about uncertainty, rejection, or failure, so we put things off.

For example, you're procrastinating about updating your resume even though you hate your job. Why? Changing jobs means leaving the protective nest of your cubicle and leaping into the unknown. You'll have to meet new people, learn new skills, and even speak in public—all of which terrifies you. While your fears are just thoughts, and there is zero threat involved in creating a new resume, the procrastination demon sits on your shoulder and weighs you down.

Here are some other examples. You want to meet the partner of your dreams, but you're procrastinating because you've had a string of bad relationships. You're worried that a new relationship will be just like the last one, leaving you heartbroken and exhausted. Or you're delaying improving your diet because you're worried that if you change your eating habits you won't be able to go out with your friends to your favorite restaurants. You don't want to be that woman who asks the waiter, "Please take away the breadbasket, serve the sauce on the side, and don't bring the dessert menu."

Fortunately, there are a number of techniques to recalibrate so you don't procrastinate. Here are some to try:

Grounding. Before you start any task, ground yourself by checking in and connecting with why accomplishing the task you're procrastinating about is important to you. Doing so will help you to stay clear and focused.

When you're stuck, grab your *Rock Your Midlife Playbook*[i] or journal and use these prompts to better understand what you want and what's holding you back:

What do I truly want?

What am I scared of?

What can I accomplish today that my future self will appreciate and love me for?

Coupling. This technique entails linking what you're procrastinating about with something you love to do. For example, you only get to listen to your favorite audiobook when you exercise. You only drink your favorite coffee while you write, pay bills, or work on the project you've been procrastinating about. You can only binge-watch your favorite show while you batch cook healthy meals or fold laundry.

Break tasks down. This is one of my favorites and something I use for all my projects, especially those that generate overwhelm. Instead of trying to tackle an entire task, break it down into manageable chunks. This can be a specific action item or a time commitment. It's great for writing reports, weeding the garden, getting in shape, or de-cluttering.

For example, you could weed one small section a day or commit to three, fifteen-minute weeding sessions a week. You could set a timer to lift weights for ten minutes or do five pushups a day. (You'll probably do more while you are down there.) For a report or book, you could commit to working on it for thirty minutes at a time or until you complete a certain number of words or pages.

This works because progress builds momentum. As you get closer to your end goal, motivation—the desire to do things—increases. In addition, the speedier you complete a productive task, the quicker your day develops into being productive and effective.

Make a to-do list. Super easy and powerful especially when it becomes a habit. At the end of your day write down the three top things you want to accomplish tomorrow. (Yes, you are putting it off for tomorrow but also committing to get it done and make it happen.) Then rank the items in terms of importance. The next day pull out your list and focus only on the first item. Commit to completing it. After you finish, cross it off and give yourself a gold star for accomplishing it, which brings us to...

Give yourself rewards. If you want to recalibrate and not procrastinate, reward yourself whenever you accomplish a task. Do something nice for yourself as soon as you finish. For example, after you do your morning workout, reward yourself with a great cup of coffee and watch or read something you enjoy. When you complete several weeks of doing something that's important to you, give yourself a bigger reward. For example, every time you go to bed by 10 p.m. draw a happy face on your calendar. When you consistently go to bed on time for 25 days, take yourself out on a date or buy yourself a little something. This will reinforce the behavior you've been procrastinating about.

Create visual cues. Tracking your progress is powerful. (Think the chore charts you may have created for your kids or the reading charts you had when you were in elementary school.) Create a visual cue to remind yourself of what you have to do and what you have already done. Every time you perform the new habit, whether it's reading for twenty minutes, staying hydrated, or meditating, mark it off on your chart.

One of my clients did this using an erasable plastic tracker that she placed on the refrigerator. Things that she'd been trying to do consistently for years magically happened within weeks of starting. Rather than beating herself up for all she wasn't doing, she felt tremendous satisfaction every time she looked at the tracker and realized how much she had accomplished.

Use the five-second rule. This one comes from author and motivational speaker Mel Robbins. It's so effective that she's written a whole book about it called, *The 5 Second Rule.* According to Robbins, you have a five-second window to act before procrastination hits. Here's Robbins' Rx: "When you feel yourself hesitate before doing something that you know you should do, count 5-4-3-2-1-GO, and move towards action."

MINDSHIFT #3: OVERCOME YOUR "IMMUNITY TO CHANGE"

In my work as a coach, I'm amazed at how many clients have one foot on the gas and one on the brake. They really want to get healthy, switch careers, start a side hustle, begin a spiritual practice, or find an amazing partner. However, instead of taking steps to make their dreams a reality, they do the exact opposite.

Why do we humans behave so bizarrely? It turns out that we literally have an *immunity to change* that keeps us stuck. Just like bodily antibodies identify and destroy pathogens, your psyche identifies and destroys the motivation to accomplish your improvement goals that compete with hidden, underlying commitments. This immune system steps in whenever some new behavior challenges opposing commitments.

Take my client, Patricia. She knew that she needed and wanted to take better care of herself, but for some reason, she never found the time to take long walks and hot baths, do yoga, or read. When we dug deep to figure out why self-care was so hard, we discovered that Patricia had a hidden commitment to be available 24/7 for her grandkids. Taking time for self-care felt selfish and self-indulgent. Plus, she liked feeling needed and indispensable. Scheduling self-care threatened that hidden commitment.

Or consider Tina, who gained over fifty pounds during the pandemic. She had asthma and was on meds for high blood pressure and high cholesterol. She knew she needed to change her lifestyle, but instead of planning meals and snacks and scheduling time to exercise, she sat all day long and ate candy bars and chips during work and ice cream late at night. What was her hidden underlying commitment? She didn't want to face the fact that she had let herself go and couldn't walk up the stairs without feeling out of breath. In addition, she was a rock star at work because she made herself available 24/7. Taking time for meals and walks, she believed, meant letting her team down.

Fortunately, there is an immunity to change process developed by Harvard psychologists Robert Kegan and Lisa Laskow Lahey, that can help you identify and overcome your transformation barriers. The process and four steps are outlined in Kegan and Lahey's book, *Immunity to Change: How to Overcome It and Unlock Potential in Yourself and Your Organization.*

Here's a summary. First, identify the specific improvement goal you want to achieve. The goal must be important to you and something you can improve upon. Next, examine the actions or lack of action that interferes with taking steps towards your goal. For example, babysitting the grandkids instead of working on your side business or practicing self-care.

Now imagine doing behaviors that are the opposite of what you just wrote down. For example, working on your side business or taking a brisk walk rather than babysitting the grandkids. What fear, sense of loss, or discomfort arises when you imagine doing the goal-achieving behavior? What's in your "worry box?" Unearthing your worries will enable you to identify your underlying commitments.

For example, if you imagine working on your side business, your worry might be: *If this doesn't work, I'll feel like a failure and look stupid.* Your underlying commitment is to never fail or look stupid. Or, if you imagine practicing self-care rather than babysitting, you may worry that you will disappoint your family. Your commitment is to always be available.

Once you understand your competing commitments, look at your underlying assumptions—the belief that helps you see why you have one foot on the gas and one on the brake. Some assumptions may be true; others may not. For example, if you are committed to always being available for your family, your big assumption may be: *If I disappoint my family, they won't love or need me.*

To determine whether or not your assumptions are correct test them in small, safe, actionable ways. For example, you spend time on your business and make a mistake. Rather than feeling like a failure or looking stupid, you realize you learned from your mistake and self-corrected or got help. Or you say no to overnight babysitting, but yes to yoga on Sunday, and notice how your kids respond. Although they may be a little annoyed, they still love you and are actually happy that you are taking care of yourself.

While the immunity to change process isn't easy, it yields big results, especially when used to get over the unconscious roadblocks that stand in the way of your big, juicy goals. It's like shining a 240-watt light on your life.

MINDSHIFT #4: FACING YOUR FEARS

Ultimately, what's really keeping you stuck is *fear*—fear of judgment, failure, and success. Yes, some people will judge you as you make needed changes and perhaps not like you, but the folks who really love and get you will support you. Making changes sorts the wheat from the chaff, revealing who really values you and has your back. Plus, as you shift you'll make new friends—allies who resonate with your new vibe and want to support you.

Sure you're scared that you may fail. Hate to break it to you, but you will. If you put yourself out there and date again, you'll smooch some frogs. If you look for a new job, you'll get rejection letters.

When you change your diet and get healthier, you're going to have a Twinkie, Twizzler, or Twix setback. Failure is part of the transformation process. Like a toddler, you get up after you go splat. That's how you learn to walk. Failure is a cornerstone of your success palace.

Fear of success: this is a strange one but something I see constantly in my coaching work. I'm amazed at how often it appears. Typically it starts with the "What ifs, as in:

"*What if* people love my paintings and buy them all. How will I keep up with all that work?"

"*What if* I start that class, business, or go back to school. How will I find the time to do the work?"

"*What if* I change my diet or stop drinking? How will I have fun with my friends and my spouse?"

"*What if* I get a great job and can't do the work?"

As I'll remind you throughout the book, your brain doesn't care about you being happy or fulfilled, let alone getting unstuck. You're brain (at least the primitive lizard part) is only focused on one thing: keeping you safe. That's why your brain has a built in switch to keep you from facing your fears and going for your dreams, which might be too dangerous.

Known as the *negativity bias,* this psychological phenomenon means that we tend to register and dwell on negative events more than positive ones. As psychologist and bestselling author of *Hardwiring Happiness,* Rick Hanson puts it, "The mind is like Velcro for negative experiences and Teflon for positive ones."

Why? We were designed to survive hundreds of thousands of years ago when if you didn't run from a hungry saber-toothed tiger, you'd get eaten. If your hunter and gatherer ancestors didn't migrate when the food supply dwindled, they'd have starved, and you wouldn't be here.

Your brain is hardwired for negativity, which is why the moment you start thinking about change, it chimes in: *Don't go there!* Change = uncertainty, and uncertainty = unsafe. Blame it on your brain.

You're living in the 21st century with a brain that was designed to function tens of thousands of years ago.

What's exciting is that you can outsmart *and* change your brain. Scientists used to think that the brain didn't change once we reached adulthood. We now know that the brain experiences *neuroplasticity*, which means that it grows, changes, and develops throughout our lifetime. In this book, I'll share the latest and greatest mental tools and techniques that you can use to change your brain so you don't keep playing the same old tapes.

What Hanson suggests is that when something good happens, savor it. When something bad happens, learn from it, and let difficulties and things you can't control go. Do more activities that you excel at and enjoy, and less of what drains you.

Here's another scientifically proven technique to help you shift towards the positive vector: *gratitude*. First, raise your arms in a victory stance. This alone will make you feel like a winner. Next, using your fingers to count, name ten things you are grateful for. Stuck? Add yourself, now you only have nine. Do this daily, and I guarantee you'll start to feel more positive and less stuck. That's because you can't be grateful and ruminate (i.e. focus on your worries and problems) simultaneously.

BABY STEPS ADD UP TO BIG CHANGE

If after looking at your tendency to ruminate and procrastinate, investigating your immunity to change, and facing your fears, you still feel stuck, take a baby step and change something. This could be as simple as parting your hair another way, wearing a bright color instead of sticking to neutrals, buying your latte at a different coffee shop, having a smoothie for breakfast instead of oatmeal, or reading *The Washington Post* instead of the *New York Times*.

> *"Insanity is doing the same thing and expecting different results."*
>
> —Albert Einstein

This works because at midlife it's incredibly easy to get locked into your routine. Doing something, anything differently fires new brain synapses and helps you let go of the daily tasks and repetition that keeps you locked in. You don't need to be Einstein to realize the need to change on some level to get different results. Making a change and doing something new on any level is like putting that piece of cardboard under your tires when you're stuck in the mud, it gives you traction so you can break free.

When you feel stuck, turn to the Appendix and choose one of the twenty-one ideas I've provided to help you make a change so you can break free.

TAP INTO COURAGE: A PATH WITH HEART

Getting unstuck and moving forward at midlife takes tremendous courage. I've been there, and I know how overwhelming and daunting it can feel. I also know how empowering it is to break through and come out the other side filled with joy, hope, and anticipation about what's next.

You can turn off your autopilot, pull yourself out of the mud, and do it too. As Mel Robbins explains in the aforementioned book, "The odds of you being born *you* are one in 400 trillion. You owe it to yourself, to humanity, to start living up to your potential."

You have a superpower in your back pocket: courage. Courage is the battering ram that will enable you to push through your comfort zone, meet challenges head-on, and break free from old habits and ways of thinking. It will help you stand up and persevere rather than stay seated when you're faced with adversity, fear, and anxiety. Courage will allow you to be vulnerable and authentic which is the first step to transforming your life and making your next chapter your best chapter.

While we think about courage as being brave, the word actually means "taking the path with heart." The word courage comes from *cour*, French for heart. Don't worry if you've forgotten how to listen to your heart. Many women have. Your inner guidance system is still there and working. It's just gotten a little rusty. I'll teach you how to knock the rust off and oil up your intuition mojo throughout the book.

By the time you reach Step 7: Enlighten Yourself, you'll be a star like Dorothy in *The Wizard of Oz*. You'll realize that not only do you have a heart (represented by the Tinman), a brain (represented by the Scarecrow), and courage (represented by the Cowardly Lion), the way home has always been inside of you.

Being courageous isn't about being fearless. Feeling fear is healthy and normal. When harnessed correctly, fear can even be helpful because, like a flashing red light, it's a signal to slow down and weigh the risks and benefits. In contrast, being frozen by fear is unhealthy, because it keeps you from facing what you need to do to grow, thrive, and rock your midlife.

One of the most powerful ways to be courageous is to analyze why you're scared and not allow fear to freeze you. Courage is the energy that will enable you to look fear in the face, plan a course of action, and move past limitation and restriction even when you're terrified. By following the path with heart, you'll see different perspectives, multiple blind spots, and know how best to move forward.

Fortunately, courage is a muscle. The more you use it, the stronger it and you become. Each time you step outside your comfort zone and take a risk, you become wiser and more self-confident and can accomplish more. You start to seek out new challenges and go for goals that are important to you.

So when you feel stuck, don't pull an Eight of Swords and stay trapped. Pull off that blindfold, take a look around, and you'll notice that the chains you thought were keeping you stuck have been loose the entire time. You have choices. Realizing that is enough to get unstuck, birth something new, and discover your authentic self, which is your first of my Rock Your Midlife seven steps you're about to learn in Part II.

PART II

TRANSFORM YOURSELF:

7 STEPS
TO ROCK YOUR MIDLIFE

3.

STEP #1: WHO AM I, REALLY? FROM CONFUSED TO AUTHENTIC

Today you are You, that is truer than true. There is no one alive who is You-er than You.

— Dr. Seuss

The week between Christmas and New Year's is always a busy time for me. At the end of the year people tend to reflect and think about the year ahead. After too much family time, holiday cheer, and eggnog, the ball drops, and many women are ready for a makeover.

December 2020 was such a time on steroids. Covid chaos was in full swing, and we were all feeling uncertain about our future. My calendar was packed with women 911-ing me for clarity, direction, and help to shed the holiday-and-stress-eating-induced muffin top.

Beth was one of them. She had signed up for a life design reading, a powerful, intuitive, informative report I offer that reveals your passion, purpose, life's work, and what you need to be healthy.

Her reading revealed she was a very sensitive person, gifted with the ability to deeply understand dynamics and be a vessel for humanity's future direction. From the reading, I expected her to be a healer, lightworker, mediator, or work for a nonprofit. What did she do for a living? She was a corporate accountant. While being an accountant is a great profession for many women, it was clearly not the right fit for Beth and out of alignment with her soul.

Super busy, struggling with demanding work she disliked, in a lackluster relationship with a truck driver, and deeply unhappy, she felt stressed and unsettled and was having trouble finding direction and motivation. Sleep was an issue, which makes sense because our souls keep us up at night when we're not at peace with who we are and the work we are doing in the world.

"I don't know what I'm passionate about," she told me as we chatted via Zoom. I still haven't figured out who I want to be when I grow up."

"That's okay," I said. "I can help you figure all of this out. Coaching can help you get there faster, with less effort, and more fun."

I invited her to go on a journey of discovery with me. She hesitated and said, "Let's talk after tax season."

I called after April 15th, but then there was another tax season to worry about, and another and another. Like many women I meet, Beth put her own transformation on hold.

"I don't want to give up what I know for the unknown," she told me.

"You're not giving anything up," I replied. "As you explore who you are and what makes you happy, you will gain so much. Yes, things will fall away, but they are all just the lampshades that are keeping your light from shining."

Ultimately, Beth was too scared to get to know herself on a deeper level and explore her authenticity because she worried that it would open up her personal Pandora's box. The unleashed demons would upset her apple cart of a life that was predictably moving along, even though it tasted like vinegar. She chose to be comfortably uncomfortable over the exploration and expansion necessary to create a deeply satisfying life.

TRANSFORMING FEAR INTO EXCITEMENT

If like Beth, you are afraid to explore who you are, that's okay. It means you're finding your Edge—a point where you're mentally and physically challenged. Facing your fears, as you learned in the last chapter, stepping outside your comfort zone and exploring your limits is exactly what you need to do to get unstuck and create the life you want.

I understand because for years I stayed small and safe and then, in the words of diarist Anaïs Nin, writing in her published journals, "The day came when the risk to remain tight in a bud was more painful than the risk it took to blossom." I took that first step, went on a journey of self-discovery, and flowered.

Feeling afraid, confused, and overwhelmed as you transform is normal. In fact, if you're afraid and uncertain, you're moving in the right direction. As you discovered in the last chapter, fear is liquid nitrogen for the mind, triggering brain freeze to keep you safe.

When you feel uncertain, afraid, or overwhelmed, acknowledge the feeling.

Realize that it's just a thought. It may be a powerful thought that's deeply rooted in your past, perhaps going back to your childhood. Unearth it. Don't let it stop you from taking the steps you need to create a life you love. Stay tuned, I'll provide more ways to manage your mind and make it your servant, not your master, in Step 4.

Once you unearth and acknowledge the inertia that arises when you contemplate change, get excited. You're about to meet yourself. Feel the energy of anticipation. It's the emotional equivalent of being a kid right before your birthday, Halloween, Christmas, or the last day of the school year. Tap into that "School's out for summer" or

"Santa's coming to town," exhilaration. That vibe will catapult you past fear, doubt, and overwhelm that can show up when you start to examine who you are.

Don't pull a Beth. Be more frightened of looking back at your life 30 years from now and regretting what you didn't do but were meant to do during this lifetime. Whether you believe in reincarnation or not, you only get one shot at being you with this personality, this past, this present, this future yet to be written. And I'm here to help. I'm going to teach you everything that I would have shared with Beth so you can figure out who you are and who you want to be.

THE STARTING POINT

Let me personally congratulate you. Unlike Beth, you've made it to Step 1.

You're about to start to truly, deeply get to know yourself.

You're in good company. Philosophers and writers from Socrates and Shakespeare to Dr. Seuss, all emphasized the importance of knowing and being true to yourself. Why is it so important? Transforming yourself and making your next chapter your best chapter begins at the "know yourself" starting line.

Don't worry if you have no idea what getting to know yourself even means, let alone how to do it. Basically, it entails understanding your strengths (yes you've got those), and your limitations and weakness (yes, you have those too; we all do). This takes courage and vulnerability. It involves discovering your passion, purpose, desires, and dreams—essentially what lights you up—as well as what turns you off. It's liberating because when you know yourself, you can say yes from the bottom of your heart and the top of your soul to the life you are creating.

Conversely, if you don't know yourself, there's no way you can create a life you love. Instead, you will generate a life that may look good on the outside, but inside it may feel bad because it's not right for you. It's like going to a shoe store and finding the perfect pair of boots—they're the right style and color, but the store only has one pair left, and it's a size seven and you're a nine. You can't change the size of your feet, and no matter what you do or how much you try to stretch the boots, they don't fit. Until you wear shoes that measure up, every step forward will hurt.

Starting today, not in an imagined future when you like yourself more, lose the weight, change jobs or partners, get out of debt or… you are going to get to know yourself in a deeper way. There's a myth out there that change is *always* a slow process. Sometimes that's true. Your life can also change in a moment, but you have to take that first step. This is it!

Do not skip this step. This is the foundation for your transformation. You can't build your next chapter without knowing who you really are. If you don't figure this out, you'll keep climbing a ladder of success, but it will be up against the wrong building. When you finally reach the destination that you've pointed your compass at, you won't be happy because it's not your North Star. Determining who you are is your North Star.

LIFE IS A THREE-RING CIRCUS

To inspire you to dig deep into the truth of who you are, let me tell you about one of my amazing clients, Veronica. When she first contacted me, Veronica was fifty-two and had numerous challenges. An entrepreneur, Veronica ran a successful, busy internet hosting company. She waited hand and foot (actually more like keyboard and mouse) on hundreds of demanding clients who required that their websites hummed 24/7.

To add to her stress, she was also the primary caregiver for her eighty-six-year-old mother who lived next door. Plus, as she put it, "I'm going through menopause with a vengeance." Mood swings were a constant companion. To feel better she'd self-medicate with a glass of wine each night to ease the stress. The nightly Chardonnay and cheddar habit had packed on the pounds and was driving her husband, a fitness nut, crazy.

She was trying to get in shape and eat right, but motivation was low, so she was mostly going through the motions. She wanted to transition out of her current business and into a new chapter, but kept getting caught up in the daily tedium and losing track. Worried about having enough money for retirement, she'd lose confidence in her plan and stop taking steps forward and making progress. Miserable inside and stuck, she wanted guidance and support to propel her into something new for her "second act" so she could feel enthusiastic about life again.

To reignite her passion for life, we looked back to Veronica's enchanting childhood. She literally grew up in an amusement park next to a circus. Summers were spent watching adults clown around and hang on the trapeze. She had even written a book called *Circus Towne* about her childhood, but now felt trapped on a haunted house Ferris wheel worrying about work and finances.

I suggested that she start to explore her love for the circus. She took up the challenge and found ways to integrate the circus vibe into her life. Since childhood, Veronica dreamed of swinging higher and being that daring girl on the flying trapeze. To make the dream a reality, she planned a circus-themed long weekend away with her husband. Prior to the event, she worked out to get her arms and abs in shape so she could hang on a bar for at least thirty seconds. She had a marvelous time and successfully crossed "be a trapeze artist" off her bucket list.

After the daring trapeze weekend, the circus fire remained in her belly. Out came the juggling balls and hula hoop. Her office decor got a circus theme makeover, and she started giving "Circus Power" talks to women's groups, businesses, and senior living communities.

The circus energy brought her to life. She stopped drinking, ate healthier, and made time to take long walks in nature and practice yoga. Now she's literally a proud Pollyanna. Not only does she look on the bright side of life, but Veronica has also created a Glad Shop in her hometown of Littleton, New Hampshire where Eleanor Porter, the author of the early 1900s classic book *Pollyanna*, lived. She's sold her internet company, and like a trapeze artist, continues to go for and catch her dreams.

TAKE AN INVENTORY:
JOURNAL YOUR WAY TO SELF-AWARENESS

Now it's your turn to learn about you. Getting to know yourself can be fun; after all, you're unique and interesting. The easiest way to do it is the same way you get to know other people: spend time with yourself, ask deep, meaningful, personal questions. Essentially, interview yourself.

I suggest you acquire a journal specifically for working with the material in this book. I'm here to support you through the discovery process and so have created a *Rock Your Midlife Playbook*[i]—a journal that is designed to help you get the most from this book. Print it out and write your answers in it to the numerous journaling prompts I provide. It will help you to get to know yourself and track your progress as you work through the seven steps for transforming yourself and your life.

Regular journaling is a powerful tool to increase self-awareness. It can also reduce stress, improve your mood and memory, and even strengthen your immune system.

Whether you're new to journaling or have been doing it for years, I suggest you block out regular time to write and make it a weekly habit. You can find a quiet, beautiful place in your home or visit a local coffee shop or library. Think of journaling as spending weekly quality time with yourself.

There are numerous ways to journal, including free association, mind mapping, letter writing, writing about a picture, and using prompts. Free association entails writing whatever comes to mind.

It's a great way to tap into your higher, wise self. Mind mapping is a great technique to gain clarity. It's done by writing down key concepts and then linking thoughts by connecting ideas with lines. Letter writing involves writing a letter that you don't intend to send. You can write to yourself or someone else in your life. It can be a wonderful way to uncover and express your feelings. You are safe to say whatever you want to yourself or another, which can improve your relationships. Writing about a picture is a powerful way to get to know yourself. You do it by selecting a picture of yourself from any time in your life. Then you write about the thoughts, feelings, and memories that arise when you look at the picture.

Using prompts involves starting with a question or sentence that spurs self-reflection. This is the method we are going to use extensively in our work together, as I provide journaling and other "laboratory" exercises at each step for you, so you can explore and experiment with the content you read. So grab your journal, and let's begin.

Preparing to journal. Whatever technique you choose, it's a good idea to empty your mind of worrisome, heavy thoughts prior to journaling. Let go of any expectations around what this experience "should" look or feel like. To clear your mind, take a few deep breaths, spend a few minutes meditating, or go for a short walk.

Don't worry if journaling is challenging. Writing may not have been your jam as a kid and digging deep may pull up painful emotions or memories. Know that everyone can write. Remember, no one else will see your words, so reassure yourself that you're safe and can do this. Pull out your journal and keep the questions rolling. Excavating old memories is a good thing. What you reveal you can heal.

Keep going. Journaling will get easier as you practice. You've got several decades to spend with yourself. When you know yourself well, you will be better able to provide for your needs and do more of what makes you happy.

ROCK YOUR MIDLIFE LAB
First date with yourself

Imagine that you're on a first date with yourself. You've discovered that you are your own soul mate, a beloved friend, and partner. Where will you go? How will you dress? What questions will you ask to unearth your unique tastes, opinions, quirks, and strengths? Get personal. Be vulnerable. Harness curiosity. Dig deep. Be present.

Here are journaling prompts to get you started on the road to knowing yourself better. I suggest starting with one question at a time and writing until the answer feels complete:

- What do you like and love?
- What do you dislike?
- What makes you angry or frustrated?
- If you could visit your seven-year-old self what would you say to her? What brings you joy?
- Given the choice of anyone in the world, who would you like to take to lunch?
- What are you grateful for?
- When do you feel most content or at peace?
- What does your perfect day look like?
- If you could change anything in the world what would it be?
- What accomplishment are you proudest of?
- When you're old and look back on your life, what do you want it to have stood for?

ROCK YOUR MIDLIFE LAB
Go back to K-12

Another way to get to know yourself is to go back to kindergarten. This is a powerful time to investigate because, at five or six, we have a big enough vocabulary to communicate needs and feelings and define ourselves within a group setting. This is the stage when we develop a strong sense of self, transition from *me* to *we* (more on this in Step 6), and start to ask big questions like, Who am I, and how do I fit in? Examining your kindergarten self can help you understand early impulses, inspirations, and visions, many of which may still ring true today.

We're wise at five. Before the world steps in and flattens us, we are buoyant and wonder-full, hungrily gobbling up all the experiences life pitches as we learn to master the world around us. Along with learning to zip and tie, we develop courage and independence. We know what we like, and our hopes and dreams for the future are often huge.

This is a great time to grab some old pictures of yourself as a kid and write about the girl you see in the photo and the thoughts, feelings, and memories that the image evokes.

You might also do this visualization exercise: Close your eyes and imagine you're five or six. See yourself as a kindergartener, sitting with your classmates on little carpet squares labeled with your initials in black Sharpie. The teacher asks, *Who do you want to be when you grow up?* What is your answer? Movie star, dress designer, president, stockbroker, veterinarian, stewardess, mother, horse trainer, librarian, electrician, or...?

Ask your younger self if there was an occupation that you saw an adult doing and said, *When I grow up I want to do or be that*? Write down in your journal what you discover.

What did your soul know way back before you were influenced by the outside world and had developed prejudices and biases? That is your seed. Connect with it. See yourself as that little girl who knew who she was and who she wanted to be when she grew up. Did you like to play with stuffed animals or cars, do puzzles, crochet, make cakes in your Easy-Bake Oven? My fiancée, Ken, spent hours as a kid playing with trucks and digging in the dirt. Now he's passionate about gardening. Nothing brings him more joy than germinating seeds, riding a tracker, and watching plants thrive in the sun.

After you consider what lit you up when you were five, step into the elementary school years. What subjects did you naturally enjoy? What shows did you like when you were growing up? Why did they interest you? What books impressed you? What games did you enjoy playing?

Then explore those high school days. Were you intrigued by history? What electives did you love? What after-school activities did you participate in? There are clues here.

To jog your memory, view additional pictures of your younger self. Be on the lookout for the ones where you look radiant and happy. Pull out your high school yearbook.

After journaling about your childhood, notice what themes emerge. What did you discover? No worries if you've gotten off track. It happens. As we grow and mature, we're influenced by parents, peers, teachers, and society and veer off course.

MY DISCOVERIES: MAGIC, MAGENTA, AND THE MACARENA

As a child, I believed in magic (still do). I knew that my favorite color was magenta (still is), my favorite food was chicken wings (still up there), and my favorite activity was dancing (still love it), any form from modern to the Macarena.

When Mrs. B, my kindergarten teacher, asked the class, "What do you want to be when you grow up?" my answer was *a writer.* I had no idea how I knew that. I didn't know much about what being a writer was or what the job entailed, but deep in my soul— before my parents, peers, and society filled me with ideas about what professions were good or bad—I had this spark of an idea. Now here I am writing and publishing my fifth book and planning my sixth, *Second Saturn Return.*

At five, I followed that marvelous breadcrumb. I loved stories, especially Greek myths, fairy tales, and Aesop's Fables. My first story, written in kindergarten, was titled "The Magic Radish." It was about a little root vegetable that granted wishes to anyone who picked him. My Aunt Barbara illustrated it for me, and my entire kindergarten class put on a play based on the story.

Along with being a writer, I wanted to be a dancer because it felt so fantastic—joyful, like flying effortlessly through a dream. However, while it was a fine childhood activity, the dancer's path as a vocation was not encouraged and nurtured by my parents. Wanting to please them, I followed a course they would approve of rather than one that lit me up.

I attended the best college I was accepted to—a large Ivy—even though it wasn't a great fit for me. Rather than discovering myself, I got stressed out figuring life out. Instead of thinking deeply, I jumped into a major (economics) and career (corporate marketing executive) that wasn't a good fit—kinda like Beth. Fortunately, I course-corrected, and you can too.

YOU'RE A ZEN KOAN

The riddle of who you are is a marvelous Zen koan. Like, "the sound of one hand clapping," koans are questions, stories, or statements used in Zen practice, a type of Buddhist tradition. The point of these puzzles is to trigger doubt and get students to think deeply about themselves and the world in order to uncover greater truths.

Stay curious. Keep dwelling on the question: Who am I? Beyond your name and all the labels you have for yourself that define your career, relationships, and nationality, who are you? Beyond judgmental thoughts of what's good and bad about you, what you like and what you don't about yourself, what you think others think about you—who are you?

Own the truth of who you are on the deepest level. You are free, you are powerful, you are good, you are love, you have value, you have purpose. Like an essential oil, this is the essence of who you are.

The truth about you is you are *authentic*. You are the *author*-ity—master, leader, author—of your life. You have the right to create a life you love.

Start with the deep koan question: *Who am I?* Ask it again and again. Let it roll around in your mind: Who am I, *really?* Here is another koan: What was your original face before you were born? When you remove all the labels you've collected like stamps—daughter, sister, wife, mother, Democrat, Republican, Black, White, Yellow, or Brown… who are you, really?

This may feel strange, uncomfortable, or slightly insane, but what I want you to do is discover the essence of who you are on a deep, soul level. When you rip off the labels and judgment calls, what's left?

Following this path, as difficult as it can be, is the way to truth and light. It is a way of understanding yourself as divine. You become part of the "I Am" presence, the answer God gave Moses at the burning bush (Exodus 3:14) when Moses asks God what to tell the

Israelites about his identity. God replies, "I am who I am." Make the song of creation part of who you are.

If that's too esoteric for you, sing the Gloria Gaynor song, "I Am What I Am," to yourself in the shower.

ADOLESCENCE AND MIDLIFE

I started asking these questions in my teens. I had this wacky English teacher, Mrs. Marshal. A heavy chain smoker, her skin was pallid yellow, and she reeked of nicotine, but her students loved her. Dark, funny, and edgy, she taught an English class that focused on existentialism, nicknamed "What the F*ck Are We Doing Here Anyway?"

Being a teen was depressing enough. Reading Camus, Sartre, and Kafka deepened the adolescent angst like a giant pimple appearing right before a first date.

Kafka's most famous work, *The Metamorphosis,* hit me hard. The novella is about a man named Gregor Samson. He wakes up one morning from troubled dreams and finds that he's been changed into a cockroach – *ungeheures Ungeziefer,* German for "monstrous vermin." I was so struck by the story that I created a six-foot-long, stuffed, batik, soft sculpture of Gregor as the cockroach, complete with six spindly legs and deep, oozing wounds inflicted on him by his family.

Stuck on his back like a helpless turtle aimlessly beating its legs in the air in an attempt to right itself, Gregor can't move from his bed. Rather than being horrified by his predicament, he ruminates about how he hates his work as a traveling salesman and the financial pressures of being his family's sole breadwinner.

While there are many ways to interpret the story, one point Kafka is making is that we can get lost in our family and job responsibilities to the point where we toil away at work we hate and feel like an insect. Gregor is so used to being mistreated and feeling bad about himself that he wakes up and is a giant bug and doesn't even notice the physical transformation.

Midlife, like adolescence, is a powerful time to ask deep, penetrating questions about yourself and your life. These two periods are marked by huge hormonal shifts that can trigger a slew of physiological and psychological changes. So many of us go through "the change," as our daughters simultaneously morph into women. This can make life both interesting and tumultuous. The men in your lives may wonder why you are both moody and difficult, especially during the full moon.

These hormonal shifts are a wake-up call telling us that our bodies and lives are transforming. It's tempting to be like Gregor, sleepwalking through life and repeating the same thing day after day. We are comfortably uncomfortable, disliking ourselves and our life and doing nothing about it. We wake up on the same side of the bed, at the same time each morning, go to the bathroom, check our phones, take a shower, make coffee, get the kids ready, go to work, come home, have a glass of wine and a meal, watch TV, snack, go to bed, and repeat the same routine week after week.

But it doesn't have to be that way. As author and neuroscientist Joe Dispenza explains in his marvelous book, *Breaking the Habit of Being Yourself:* "You are not doomed by your genes and hardwired to be a certain way for the rest of your life." There is a new science emerging that empowers all human beings to create the reality they choose.

In the chapters ahead, you'll discover not only who you are, but who you want to be. By following this trail, guided by your North Star, you'll discover how to manifest a life that feels good in your body and soul.

DISCOVER YOUR STRENGTHS

If someone asked you to define your top strengths, what would you say? Not sure? After you do a thorough inventory and uncover your personal preferences through the journaling exercises I've provided, consider your strengths—what you naturally excel at. Doing so can help you be more successful at work and increase life satisfaction and wellbeing.

While knowing what you excel at is vitally important for creating an authentic, meaningful, joyful life, few women take the time to investigate what they are naturally good at. Knowing and nurturing your strengths and using them to help others helps boost your confidence and resilience. Discovering your strengths feeds the motivation that will enable you to attain your long-term dreams and goals, and get back on track when you face a setback. Feeling confident and motivated in turn fuels competence, which attracts opportunities and creates more success.

Note: strengths are not the opposite of weaknesses. Trying to fix your flaws never produces positive results. Rather, it can lead to frustration and manifesting what you don't want because fixing keeps you focused on what you're not good at or don't like about yourself. Instead of trying to fix your flaws to accomplish your goals, look for people who naturally complement you. Find folks who excel where you don't and allow them to be part of your efforts. It's a win-win because you'll probably find that you have strengths that they don't.

For example, I'm great at strategic thinking and influencing others. However, I suck at execution. No matter how hard I try, I'm disorganized and have trouble finishing projects. I used to beat myself up because I had trouble completing things. Then I embraced my strengths and weaknesses and hired coaches and assistants who were good at implementation. I do more of what is in my genius zone, staying in flow (the state where you lose track of time because you are challenged and enjoying what you're doing) and less of what frustrates me and I'm not naturally good at.

ROCK YOUR MIDLIFE LAB
Finding your strengths

I'll share some of my favorite strength assessments in a moment, but before we go there I'd like you to create your own list. Pull out your journal or *Rock Your Midlife Playbook*[i] and write down *everything* you are naturally good at. Ditch the "be humble" voices, and let curiosity reign. Here are some prompts to help:

- What you are naturally good at and love doing?
- What projects energize you and what would you work on all day long if you could?
- Where do you grow and glow when challenged?
- What motivates you?
- When do others ask you for help?
- What can you do over and over again brilliantly?
- When are you in flow, the state where you lose track of time because you are both challenged and have to stretch your skills and abilities to reach higher?
- What have others complimented you on?

Keep the list going. Add to it. Carry it so that you can pull it out when you need encouragement and want to feel good about yourself.

When you have a hefty list, show it to a good friend, your partner, or a mentor and see what they have to say. Ask them what they see as your strengths and add these qualities to the list. Aim to have three to five people that know you very well and whose opinions you trust help you with your list.

ROCK YOUR MIDLIFE LAB
Assessing your strengths

Martin Seligman, the father of positive psychology, defines strengths as the "route" through which we achieve virtues in life. Each of us has "signature virtues" that can be used in the service of something greater than ourselves. As Seligman explains in his book, *Authentic Happiness: Using the New Positive Psychology to Realize Your Potential for Lasting Fulfillment,* "The good life is using your signature strengths every day to produce authentic abundant gratification. When wellbeing comes from engaging our strengths and virtues, our lives are imbued with authenticity."

In the book *Character Strengths and Virtues,* Seligman and fellow psychologist Christopher Peterson identify twenty-four key character strengths. Each strength falls into one of six broad virtue categories—wisdom, courage, humanity, justice, temperance, and transcendence. Everyone has all twenty-four character strengths but in different amounts. The strengths range from appreciation of beauty and excellence to zest.

My top strength is spirituality, followed by curiosity and self-regulation. This makes total sense because I'm deeply interested in finding the higher purpose and meaning of the universe (I'm a Sagittarius.) I love to explore and discover, both characteristics of curiosity. I'm very disciplined especially around taking care of my body and naturally share this strength with others who have trouble with self-regulation.

There are numerous assessments available that will

help you understand yourself and identify your strengths. Here are some of my favorites:

- The VIA Institute Character Strengths Test[2] - This is where you are able to determine the twenty-four strengths identified by Seligman and Peterson. I have all my clients take this free assessment when we start working together.
- Clifton Strengths Finder - This test looks at a range of personality traits and attributes. It is available at a small cost. You can also purchase the book StrengthsFinder 2.0 which includes an access code to take the Clifton Strengths assessment.
- The Wingfinder by Red Bull[3] - This is a free, fun assessment that explores four factors: connections, drive, thinking style, and creativity. It takes about thirty minutes.
- High 5 Test[4] - This is a free test that takes about fifteen minutes. It will enable you to determine your top five strengths across four different areas.

IKIGAI: FINDING YOUR PASSION AND PURPOSE

One of the goals of all this self-exploration you are doing is to discover your passion and purpose in life. Knowing your passion and purpose will help you focus and become more fulfilled, successful, and confident. It will give you direction so you stop floundering, struggling, and getting nowhere and instead have a life that flows with grace, beauty, and ease.

Having a strong sense of purpose fuels your internal engine. It gets you out of bed in the morning and propels you forward. Your purpose enables you to find value and meaning from your life experiences and make intentional decisions. The more purpose you inject into your life, the brighter your internal spark, the more productive you'll be, and the longer and deeper you'll live.

The Japanese have a name for following your purpose. They call it *ikigai (* 生□甲斐 *)*. *Ikigai* literally means "referring to life" *(iki)* and the realization of what you expect and hope for *(gai)*. Your ikigai is where your passion, mission, profession, and vocation intersect. It's where what you love to do, do well, get paid to do, and what the world needs all come together. In Okinawa, a part of Japan where people live exceptionally long lives, *ikigai* is why you get up in the morning and enjoy the day.

The first step to finding your *ikigai* is to identify your core values— what orients you in life. Your core values are unique. They're an internal GPS, guiding you through life. Once you've uncovered your core values, you can turn them into a vow or value statement and use that statement to help direct your life.

Examples of core values include love, vitality, humor, ecology, art, adventure, generosity, peace, education, open-mindedness, courage, success, connection, hope, growth, intimacy, health, freedom, fun, creativity, meaningful connection, acceptance, compassion, significance, family, happiness, faith, patience, intelligence, and wisdom.

Not only will knowing your core values guide you through life, it will also help you stick to your goals. For example, one of my clients, Tammy, came to me because she wanted to lose weight. She'd tried countless times before and would always drop a few pounds and then gain them back. The key to success was connecting her desired outcome (lose weight) with her values, which included family, wellness, and confidence. When she realized eating right and exercising would be a good example for her son, increase her wellness, and build confidence, she was finally able to change her lifestyle for good.

ROCK YOUR MIDLIFE LAB
Discover your core values

Grab your journal or *Rock Your Midlife Playbook*[i] because I'm going to share the five-step process I use with all my clients to help them discover their core values.

1. **Brainstorm.** Think about what's important to you. Write down what you value— freedom, strength, courage, connection, compassion. Imagine it's the end of your life and you're looking back to today. What would you have liked your life to have stood for?

   Next list all your strengths that you discovered earlier in this chapter and the strengths of people you admire. Don't censor yourself. Relax and remain open. Be curious.

2. **Select.** Once you have a list of values and strengths, narrow down the list. Take your time and spend a few days with this step. Look over your list and pick the six or seven words that resonate with you. Ask yourself: What values excite me? Or: If I had to live my life guided by one of these values, which would I choose? Notice how you feel when you connect with them.

   Don't be afraid to commit. The values that shape your life are like clothing. You can try them on and take them off as you grow and change. Just like you get training and increase your qualifications for a job position, you can change your values to help you better qualify for your life purpose.

Once you've selected six to seven values, write them down, memorize them, and watch your world start to transform.

3. **Define.** Take your top three values and define what they mean to you. For example, if you selected success, ask: What does success mean to me? Or, How will I know when I've been successful? If health is a core value, define what being healthy means to you—having more energy, glowing skin, eating right, or getting a good report from your doctor.

Once you've selected six to seven values, write them down, memorize them, and watch your world start to transform.

4. **Act.** Now use your top values to determine what actions to take so your life, relationships, and work reflect your core values. For example, if you selected family, you might decide to spend more time with your kids, be more patient and really listen to them, eat meals together more often, help your daughter with her homework, or go out on a date with your spouse.

Each week select an action you will take to help you live by your core values. When you complete an action, write it down so that you can track how effectively you're living according to your core values. For example, one of my core values is creativity, so every day I write three pages in my journal and an original post for my social media feeds. I also work on my creativity by reading books on the topic. Another of my values is spirituality, so each morning I meditate, pray, and ask for guidance.

5. **Create a personal mantra.** Select one value that you'd like to have more of and turn it into a mantra or affirmation. For example: I am _____ (fill in your value), or I am experiencing more _____ (fill in value). To manifest this value in your life, keep saying it in the present tense and feel it as if it's already happening. Repeat your mantra every morning and before you go to sleep at night.

JUST JUMP

When it comes to portraying women authentically, Hollywood used to get it wrong, particularly in major popular films, and especially live-action movies directed by men. Fortunately, remarkably strong women *and* even powerful Disney princesses are becoming the norm.

Thelma and Louise is one film that departed early on from this older, sorry norm. Originally marketed as a lighthearted female buddy movie, *Thelma and Louise* was actually a groundbreaking film about female empowerment. Like so many buddy and road trip movies, the two lead characters undergo a rite of passage where they discover themselves and go from confused to authentic.

The two women in the film are ordinary, working-class girlfriends from a small town in Arkansas. Louise, played by Susan Sarandon, is a waitress who hides her traumatic past and who she truly is. Thelma, played by Geena Davis, is a housewife who is expected to be mediocre and be happy about it. They are both shoved into a subservient position, told this is all they are supposed to be, and encouraged to remain stuck.

They go on a road trip for the weekend to have some fun and get away from the men in their lives. Events unfold, and these ordinary women become extraordinary outlaws. They feel alive, strong, courageous, and authentic, and we are with and rooting for them. There is no turning back. In the end, they literally drive off a cliff, which is a metaphor for obtaining the freedom and liberation they crave.

Thirty years later, the movie is still powerful because we all crave that sense of authenticity, freedom, and adventure. Fortunately, you don't have to jump off a cliff like Thelma and Louise did to obtain it.

> *"Life is either a daring adventure or nothing at all."*
>
> —Helen Keller

You *do* have to jump out of the old, automatic ways of doing things and into the arms of the authenticity that is your birthright. You have to let go of who you think you're supposed to be and discover who you are. You do have to up-level your mindset, reach higher, and expect more of yourself.

Know that like the audience who is rooting for Thelma and Louise, I'm rooting for you. In the next chapter, Step 2, you are going to learn how to root for yourself.

CHAPTER SUMMARY:

- Being scared is normal and a sign that you are on the right track. Transform your fear into excitement!
- Create a regular journaling practice to discover who you really are. For easy access to all the prompts in this book, download your *Rock Your Midlife Playbook*[i].
- Discover your strengths.
- Define your Ikigai, your passion and purpose, and use it to guide your actions as you transform your life.

4

STEP #2: BEFRIEND YOURSELF: FROM SELF-LOATHING TO SELF-LOVE

Love yourself first and everything else falls into line.
You really have to love yourself first
to get anything done in this world.

— Lucile Ball

Figuring out who you are leads to deepening your relationship with yourself. So how is your relationship with yourself? It's a question that I ask new clients all the time. The usual response is either a shoulder shrug and "Great question. I never really thought about it." Or a grimace accompanied by "Not good."

Your relationship with yourself is the most important relationship you will ever have. From the moment you are born to the moment you leave the planet, you're with yourself. Partners, parents, children, friends will come and go, but you'll spend on average about thirty thousand days with yourself. There is no escaping spending time with you. You can't hide or ghost yourself. From first to last breath, you're gifted with about forty-three million minutes to be with you, so it's a good idea to get to know who you are and enjoy the relationship.

My own relationship with myself, however, was anything but enjoyable. Before I learned to befriend myself, it was fraught with self-criticism and self-loathing.

MY MIDLIFE DEPRESSION

"You have clinical depression," my doctor told me, grabbing an Rx pad. "I think we should treat you immediately with antidepressants," he said, scribbling a prescription for Celexa.

This was about fifteen years ago, and at the time, the diagnosis was a relief. I had an illness, not a weakness. The hopelessness, lack of productivity, and low self-esteem I had been experiencing weren't my fault. The diagnosis was due to genetics and environment. With a mind label, I could treat the depression and perhaps escape the heavy emotional blanket that had shrouded me for so many years.

I suffered and struggled with depression for decades, but was scared to name it, call it out, and shine a light on my chemically imbalanced brain. Depression was something other people had, not me. I thought I could control, overcome, or manage my mood. I didn't want to admit that I had mental health issues. Acceptance felt like failure. Wasn't I strong, spiritual, and smart enough to vaporize the muddy moods that haunted me for weeks?

Denying depression was an unhealthy strategy that bolstered my self-image and allowed me to press ahead. With caffeine as fuel and alcohol as a coping mechanism, I'd stress my adrenals to function and end the day with two fingers of scotch to wind down.

Midlife and Depression

For many women at midlife, depression is an unwelcome exit strategy. After trying to do it all and ignoring our own needs to care for others, depression is a forced STOP sign that can feel like the only way to slow down. It's an escape hatch, the body and mind's way of forcing you to hit the brakes, rest, and finally prioritize yourself—or else.

One important fact to remember is that women at midlife are at a greater risk of depression than any other group based on age and gender. According to the Centers for Disease Control and Prevention (CDC), women between forty and fifty-nine have the highest rate of depression: 12.3 percent or about one in eight. In turn, depression is associated with memory problems, confusion, and difficulty focusing and thinking clearly.

Researchers aren't sure if the high depression rates are due directly to perimenopausal-related hormonal changes or symptoms like hot flashes, insomnia, and low energy levels associated with the changes. Studies have found that after controlling for age, marital status, education, income, smoking, and menopause symptoms, perimenopause is still significantly associated with depression in midlife women. Throw in stressful life events so common at midlife—like a health crisis, divorce, or losing a parent—and you have a recipe for depression.

If you are experiencing excessive sadness, loss of interest in things you once enjoyed, low motivation, and these feelings have persisted for weeks, you may have depression. Talk with your doctor. Depression is an illness, not a weakness of character, and it can be treated in a variety of ways including therapy, behavior change, and medication.

Once my ex and I canned The Cooking Couple, the wind that had sailed us to a happy island of creativity and connection vanished. The five-course dinners at five-star restaurants and glamorous book tours evaporated. We became an unhappy couple. My people-pleasing and low self-esteem coupled with poor boundaries and communication were a recipe for codependency. Despite the fact that I thought I was a feminist, I always put my ex-husband's needs first. I strived and struggled to please him, and blamed myself when he was grouchy or negative.

With two little kids that I loved dearly, a packed schedule of personal training clients, and a three-bedroom house to clean, there was always work to do, and no time for downtime and much-needed self-care.

I was exhausted, sad, and depressed. Like so many women at midlife juggling kids and a career, the resentment brewed until sometimes I boiled over like Vesuvius, spewing lava at my helpless toddlers. I'd scream, break a glass, and feel shattered. Other times I'd shove down the anger, loneliness, and sadness and choke back the pain.

The daily bouts I had with my ex brought on the familiar darkness. I would bring him coffee, and fifteen minutes later we were at it again—fighting about anything, everyone, and everything from in-laws, kids, and finances to what to make for dinner, like I even cared about whether we had chicken or fish.

He'd get angry, and my response? Rather than telling him to calm down or walking away, I'd apologize again and again for what I'd done. I'd blame his fury on myself. As if everything that was wrong with our marriage and life was my fault.

"I'm so sorry, I'll work harder, I'll get better, I promise…"

Then I'd walk up the winding flight of stairs to my office, spent and exhausted, incapable of rubbing two sentences together let alone finishing a PhD and coaching clients. This continued for years.

I should have questioned the relationship from the start and realized it was toxic. I met my ex in my late twenties and was looking for a man to marry. He was funny and charming, handsome, and smart. We liked the same music and wanted similar things—kids and a house in the suburbs, nice vacations, and romantic dinners. He seemed to be everything I wanted in the husband department. Plus, there was strong sexual chemistry. So I ignored the red flags or, perhaps in a weird way, welcomed them because the caustic behavior and energy between us were familiar.

Like many couples, my parents sometimes fought. Still together and in love, bickering is one way they relate and communicate. As an empath and highly sensitive child, I didn't understand that. My five-year-old self was disturbed and confused by the conflicts I witnessed. Hands over ears, I'd hide in the closet for hours, bolstered by a pile of stuffed animals and wrapped in Nitto, my security blanket. No one noticed I had disappeared.

I suffered silently. I was a good little girl doing everything I could from earning A's to getting into an Ivy League college to keeping the peace at home and winning my parents' approval and love. Success was more important than acceptance. Unconditional love, from others and for myself, was a foreign concept. Back then parents, not kids, were the center of the family universe. Mom or dad told you what to do, and you did it or you got in trouble.

Like I had done with my parents, I thought if I was good, worthy, and smart enough, I would win my ex's approval and love. If I worked harder, earned a PhD, made more money, cleaned the house until it sparkled, took care of the kids, let him do what he wanted vocationally, made beautiful meals, I'd be worthy of love, and the shattering would stop.

I'd double down on the criticism by adding a dose of self-loathing to the mix, pummeling myself for making mistakes that angered him. Self-criticism was a rusty, shield for his anger. I believed if I shredded myself first, I would beat him to the punch and be bullet-proof when I experienced being criticized.

WHAT DOESN'T WORK

Activating your own self-critic to avoid another's criticism is a common but completely ineffective strategy. Yet it's widespread, particularly for women at midlife who are people pleasers focused more on the wellbeing of others than their own.

The self-critic is the internalized voice of our early caregivers that tells us we must clean our room, do well in school, finish the food on our plate, *and* be thin. Developed in childhood and shaped by how we are spoken to, our self-critic means well and is trying to help us be more successful and stay safe. She believes that if we don't follow the dictates of our caregivers, we are in danger of not being cared for and loved. To help us avoid embarrassment and shame, the inner critic tries to correct our behavior when we do something wrong. However, typically she goes overboard, pummeling us with ugly, shaming, faultfinding self-talk.

At midlife, the self-critic can become a hard shell that keeps us from growth and authenticity. She's like the Enjoli woman's evil twin. You may remember her, the twenty-four-hour woman who wore the eight-hour perfume, a sexy blond who appeared in the eighties' TV commercial. She told us to be superwoman and put our needs last. According to her, we could do it all: bring home the bacon, fry it up in a pan, never let him forget he's a man, work till five o'clock, come home, cook, and read to the kids—all in high heels while remaining perfectly coifed.

Although the commercial is over forty years old, it's still lodged in our brains along with the idea that we should take care of everyone and everything before we take care of ourselves. When we fail at being superwoman, our self-critic whips us into shape.

Rather than motivating you to change, self-criticism generates cortisol and shuts you down. Every time you activate your inner critic, you become both the victim and the bully—your own worst enemy.

Until you make friends with your self-critic and even thank her for trying to protect you, your fearful, five-year-old self will try to control your behavior because she believes that if you aren't perfect, you'll be rejected and abandoned. To heal, you must accept your imperfections, shine a light on your inner critic, and reassure your inner child that she is safe and loved.

UNLOCKING MY CAGE

During my forties, I felt like a caged tiger, trapped in my toxic marriage and the need to be perfect, pacing the floor of my cell, lacking the courage and energy to open the door and walk away. Like so many women at midlife, I was comfortably uncomfortable. The bars keeping me stuck were my thoughts, primarily fears, and the shell of a self I had created to keep me safe. What if I ended my marriage, who would love me? How would I survive? What would happen to the kids?

I knew that once I crossed the line and asked for a divorce there would be no going back. So I stayed and prayed. When the time is right and you've reached the breaking point, what you need most in life shows up. This is what happened to me.

The answer to my prayers was a surprising liberator: self-compassion, which is essentially treating yourself like a good friend. The practices I learned changed my relationship with myself. Once transformed, I could no longer do things or be in relationships that insulted my soul.

I was working on my PhD in psychology. I had gone back to grad school because I wanted to be a smarter version of Jillian Michaels, the famous personal fitness trainer and reality TV star best known for whittling contestants down physically and verbally in the show *The Biggest Loser.*

I wanted to become a psychologist, so I could combine my training as a registered dietitian nutritionist, life coach, and personal fitness trainer with behavioral change techniques. I wanted to teach women how to change their habits and lose weight because I'd been taught that everyone can and should be skinny.

Prior to grad school, I believed the self-loathing I heaped on my body was necessary to motivate me to work out and watch every calorie. Obsessively focusing on my weight and appearance were distractions that kept me from making real, meaningful changes. When something was going wrong in my life or I was struggling with difficult emotions, I dumped everything into the "I feel fat bucket." Unlike other life issues, controlling my weight felt concrete. Being skinny was something that I was good at and knew how to do.

It's a strategy that I see in many of the women I work with. They focus on weight loss instead of life change. Ironically, they often turn to food and alcohol as a way of coping with life situations that make them unhappy which packs on the pounds. In an insane diet spiral, they restrict, binge, and punish themselves by restricting again.

To make things worse, they put life on hold until they are thin. "I'll switch jobs, start to date, go to the beach, join a gym, start that business—after I lose the weight. That's why now when I work with a client, we start by elevating self-love, and everything—body image, health, love life, leisure, career, and even eating behavior—falls in place.

Ironically, one reason I became a dietitian was that I believed that if I knew more about diet and weight, I'd be able to make peace with my body and food. But learning how to count grams of fat, protein, and carbohydrates, and estimate total daily calories only made my obsession with diets and thinness worse.

Fortunately, my thinner-is-better and weight-loss-is-the-way-to-happiness mindset did a 180 in grad school. While working on my doctorate, I had a revelation: the media brainwashes women. It generates self-loathing by convincing us that to be beautiful and acceptable we must be thin and young. We internalize these impossible beauty standards. When we don't measure up, we experience negative body image and body dissatisfaction. The media then sells us products and services that address our beauty woes and promise to make us feel better.

When your appearance doesn't mirror the beauty ideal, even after you buy wrinkle creams, Spanx (which some doctors say can cause acid reflux, heartburn, and can make it hard to breathe properly), and slimming pills, shame seeps in. To make matters worse, women in our culture are taught that the most important thing about us is our looks. Rather than saying the media is wrong and manipulative, we turn the judgment around and say we are bad or unacceptable.

Negative body image – it's not just a problem for young women

Negative body image is a curse created by our culture that is central to the development of eating pathology. It's also associated with higher levels of depression and anxiety, lower self-esteem, poorer quality of life, and unhealthy behaviors such as smoking. In the words of Paul Gilbert and Jeremy Miles, authors of *Body Shame,* "When people experience their physical bodies as in some way unattractive, undesirable, and a source of a 'shamed self,' they are at risk of psychological distress and disorders."

Negative body image, along with dieting, is a major source of suffering among women of all ages that persists across the life span—thank you midlife wrinkles, age spots, and menopausal spread. Complicated, and more about your perception than reality, body image is a visual, mental, emotional, sensual, and historical problem. Weighing or appraising your naked body first thing in the morning as you step on the scale can determine how you feel about yourself during the rest of your day.

We don't outgrow bad body image at midlife. A 2012 study published in the *Journal of Women and Aging* of 1,800 women over fifty found that almost 64 percent thought about their weight every day. Another 79 percent felt that their body shape or weight played a moderate to important role in self-concept. Additional research on middle-aged women published in 2014 in the *Archives of Women's Mental Health* found that 47 percent of subjects said they were dissatisfied with their appearance, and 73 percent were somewhat unsatisfied with their weight. Research published in 2010 in the *International Journal of Eating Disorders* has shown that women are least satisfied with their bodies at age fifty-four. This makes sense, given that as women hit midlife, they simultaneously move away from the cultural youthful ideal and experience undesirable body changes. Lean muscle mass decreases as the waistline expands, and hair thins and grays.

Fortunately, self-compassion can help. My dissertation research, published in the journal *Mindfulness*, which involved over five hundred women from across the globe showed that, compared to controls, women who listened to self-compassion meditations for about an hour a week had a significant reduction in body shame, body dissatisfaction, and self-worth based on appearance. In addition, both self-compassion and body appreciation improved.

I became obsessed with these innocuous-looking yet sinister messages used to sell magazines and products and to control women. I wanted to be an agent of change. My academic advisor, Stacey, felt the same way.

We started doing research on women's magazines and the "magic bullet" solutions they used to sell their publications. You know the ones. They're shelved at the checkout counter above the Dove bars and packages of Extra gum, next to the single-serving bags of Smartfood. While waiting in line and wondering if you should really buy that bag of chips or pint of cookie dough, you can't miss them. They're covered with too-good-to-be-true headlines like:

Lose 19 lbs in 10 days!

Autoslim to Your Happy Weight!

TOO HUNGRY TO LOSE WEIGHT? Breakthrough plan turns off appetite as it brings a "dead" metabolism back to life!

They know all our midlife woes and promise solutions in bold print for everything from reversing Alzheimer's to improving sleep:

NO MORE ACHEY KNEES!

TIREDNESS CURE

HEAL YOUR THYROID!

Doing this before bed boosts immunity for 133% STRONGER VIRUS DEFENSE!

The headlines, which often appear alongside pictures of Dr. Oz and scrumptious cakes, are so outlandish that they're almost laughable, but they sell magazines. *Woman's World* is one of the most popular newsstand magazines. Between the covers are recipes for comfort foods (chocolate chip cupcakes, flakey chicken pot pie, Instant Pot sticky ribs) *and* unsustainable, low-calorie, restrictive diets that will leave you so hungry, you want to eat your cat! The message is clear: you can have your cake and be thin too.

For my dissertation, I wanted to offer women a sustainable solution, something that would truly help them feel better about their bodies and themselves.

"Why don't you study meditation," Stacey suggested. As a psychologist who regularly meditated and practiced yoga, Stacey knew the mental and physical benefits of meditation, including a reduction in stress, anxiety, and chronic pain. She felt that meditation might be a virtually risk-free, cost-effective practice that, unlike the magic-bullet,

BS solutions hawked by women's magazines, could actually help women truly feel better about their bodies and themselves. Could finding inner peace reduce body-hatred and change how women perceive their appearance?

My first thought was, no way. I didn't go to grad school to teach meditation. I went to grad school to help people lose weight, but now that my thinking had flipped, perhaps teaching meditation wasn't such a bad option.

Stacey persisted, and I needed a dissertation topic. I started doing research and networking to see if I could find a type of meditation that would support women particularly around improving body image and reducing body shame.

Motivated to help reverse the ubiquitous, bad body image curse, I started googling. Using search terms like *meditation, psychology,* and *self-care,* I found Christopher Germer, a clinical psychologist and leading expert on mindfulness and compassion-based psychotherapy. I emailed Chris. Responding quickly, he suggested that I contact his colleague, self-compassion pioneer and researcher, Kristin Neff.

I reached out to Kristin, who agreed to be on my dissertation committee. Later she offered to help me publish my study on "Body Dissatisfaction and Self-compassion in Women" but on one condition: I had to take the Mindful Self-compassion training.

THE TRANSFORMATIVE POWER OF SELF-COMPASSION

I took a break from conducting my research to attend a five-day, intensive Mindful Self-compassion course taught by Kristin and Chris at Omega Institute in Rhinebeck, New York. And intense it was. Our classroom was next to Omega's Eco Machine, a water reclamation system that cleans all the water from Omega's campus (about 52,000 gallons per day from toilets, showers, and sinks), naturally using microscopic algae, fungi, bacteria, plants, and snails.

*Happiness is not dependent on circumstances being
exactly as we want them to be, or on ourselves being
exactly as we'd like to be. Rather, happiness stems from
loving ourselves and our lives exactly as they are.*

—Kristin Neff

As a result, the classroom smelled like sewage, which was appropriate, as we were processing our own refuse—the sorrows, sadness, and regrets accumulated over a lifetime. Just as the foul wastewater was turned into life-giving fuel for the plants and animals, we were learning how to productively work with and regulate our difficult emotions. To paraphrase musician Peter Gabriel, we were digging in the dirt and finding the places we had gotten hurt. Instead of snails and bacteria, we digested our "soul sludge" and alchemized it into healthy, positive energy with Mindful Self-compassion practices like *Soothing Touch, Affectionate Breathing,* and *Loving-Kindness.*

While it didn't happen overnight, practicing self-compassion transformed me and ultimately my life. I became aware of my own suffering, and instead of ignoring my pain, I soothed and comforted myself. Rather than pushing difficult emotions away or exercising to the point of exhaustion so I felt nothing, I learned to process difficult emotions including sadness, anger, and fear. When my ex yelled at me, instead of apologizing *again,* hand-on-heart I walked away and took a self-compassion break. I fired my self-critic and changed my self-talk. Self-limiting, judgmental, or destructive thoughts were exchanged for kinder, more supportive ones.

Self-compassion became my life raft and a parachute. It kept me afloat through dark periods and enabled me to fly when faced with fear, challenges, and change.

Healing myself was an act of self-love that resulted in me loving and valuing myself more than I had imagined was possible. And the negative body image? It disappeared, replaced by tremendous appreciation for everything my body does for me.

I promise; self-compassion will do the same thing for you.

THE HOW-TO OF SELF-LOVE

Throughout it all, self-compassion was my savior. It can be yours, too. What's cool is that you don't need a hero outside of yourself. You are your own liberator.

To me, self-compassion is the "how-to" of self-love. Self-love isn't just about getting massages and mani-pedis and lighting lavender candles, although these can be nice ways to practice self-care and love yourself. Treating yourself like a good friend especially when you are suffering is how you deeply love yourself. When you're hurting you've always got a good friend to call on—yourself—not to make the pain go away, but just because you're experiencing pain.

While we typically think about self-compassion as yin and nurturing, it also has a yang element that Kristin Neff describes as a fierce mother bear defending her cubs. This supportive side protects, promotes, and motivates us when we feel threatened or stuck.

Don't worry if you're struggling with self-love or self-compassion. You're not alone. Most women have trouble loving themselves and giving themselves what they need. But it's a shame because love is a powerful force and the highest vibration on the planet. It generates energy, increases wellbeing, and elevates your vibe so you can rise above fear, negativity, and uncertainty. When you're in love, you feel amazing—beautiful, connected, balanced, blessed. You wake up energized, joyful, and excited to start your day.

And love is free, abundant, and always available. Regardless of your relationship status, you can be in love 24/7—deeply, madly, passionately in love with yourself. You don't need the perfect mate or partner to feel loved, nourished, and whole. The only person who can fill your inner void and solve your problems is you.

If self-love is so glorious, why is loving ourselves so challenging? One of the main reasons is we're taught that self-love and self-care are selfish. We put everyone and everything else first—our job, spouse, house, kids, the dog. When we do find a little me time, we're too tired or feel too guilty to enjoy it.

The search for self-love can also be backward. We think that if we change ourselves and are finally perfect, then we'll love ourselves. The truth is that you can start to love yourself exactly as you are, starting now.

ROCK YOUR MIDLIFE LAB
Exploring self-love

Self-love means many different things because each of us is unique, and we all have different ways we'd like to love and care for ourselves. Grab your journal or *Rock Your Midlife Playbook*[i] and take some time to write about what self-love means to you.

Here are some ideas to get you started: notice what resonates with you:

- Accepting and appreciating yourself exactly as you are today, not in some future time when you finally lose the weight, find the perfect mate, get a promotion, get out of debt, finish that degree or...
- Prioritizing your health, happiness, and wellbeing
- Not settling for less than you need, want, and deserve.
- Being easy with yourself.
- Paying attention to your feelings.
- Fulfilling your emotional needs.
- Forgiving yourself when you screw up.

- Taking action that supports your physical, mental, emotional, and spiritual growth.
- Practicing radical self-care. Not leaning into your people pleaser at the expense of your wellbeing.
- Setting boundaries (more on this in Step 6).
- Asking others for what you need and want.

WABI-SABI YOUR WAY TO SELF-ACCEPTANCE

As you've probably discovered in Step 1, it's tempting to avoid taking a good look at yourself and your life. Flaws and cracks will appear, but you'll also discover, to paraphrase from "Anthem," a song by Leonard Cohen, there is a crack in everything, and that's how the light gets in.

Your flaws are what make you unique, bright, and beautiful. Own and celebrate them, even the mistakes. Learn from them. Heal what's hurting with a balm of self-compassion.

Wabi-sabi yourself! Wabi-sabi is a tradition of aesthetics in Japan and world-view that emphasizes seeing and appreciating beauty that is imperfect, impermanent, and incomplete. "Wabi" means simplicity, and "sabi" means beauty of age and wear. In this tradition, chipped and broken antique bowls are valued more than perfect, new ones.

As you contemplate who you are, keep this question in mind: What if I prized and appreciated my wear and tear—the imperfections and the messy cracks in my life? In this age of Botox brows, sleek cellphones, and shiny blowouts, abandoning "perfect" is powerful. Why fit in when you can stand out! Embrace your crow's feet, age spots, and scars. See genius in a gnarled tree. Enjoy the complex flavors of a lumpy heirloom tomato. If you bake a cake and it falls, turn it into a trifle.

As you've learned in this chapter, being imperfect and not living up to your ideal is a normal part of being human. The imperfections and failures hold the lessons that you need to love, heal, and grow.

Accepting all of you, the diamonds and the mud, is the path to freedom and happiness.

WHAT IS SELF-COMPASSION?

Don't worry if you have no idea how to start practicing self-compassion. Self-compassion can be learned. It's like a muscle, the more you use it the stronger it gets. No matter what you're going through (and at midlife, it's often a lot), it can help you process difficult emotions, cope, and grow stronger and more resilient.

As Chris Germer, author of *The Mindful Path to Self-Compassion: Freeing Yourself From Destructive Thoughts and Emotions,* puts it, "A moment of self-compassion will change your day. A string of these moments will change the course of your life."

Although it is magical due to its transformational power, self-compassion isn't metaphysical woo-woo. It's a scientifically sound practice backed by thousands of research articles. Self-compassion is strongly linked to less depression, anxiety, and stress and more happiness, life satisfaction, and optimism. Struggling with emotional eating or recovering from an eating disorder? Self-compassion can help you care for your feelings, so you won't want to eat them.

When practiced over time, self-compassion will enable you to understand, accept, and support yourself the way you would a good friend. Plus, anyone can learn self-compassion, even women who have an inner critic that resembles Ursula from *The Little Mermaid.*

According to self-compassion researcher and pioneer Kristin Neff, self-compassion has three components:

- *Self-kindness:* You treat yourself with care and understanding rather than harsh self-criticism or judgment. It's important to note that there is an action component here. The word *compassion* means "to suffer with," so practicing self-compassion entails actively comforting and soothing yourself when you are suffering.
- *Common Humanity:* You acknowledge that everyone suffers,

makes mistakes, and is perfectly imperfect. When suffering arises, rather than thinking that something has gone wrong, you acknowledge that this is a normal part of the human condition. As a result, you don't feel so alone.

- *Mindfulness.* You notice when you are stressed or suffering. Rather than ignoring your suffering, plowing forward, and problem-solving or ruminating, you turn towards your painful feelings with acceptance and apply a self-compassion bandage.

STARTING YOUR SELF-COMPASSION PRACTICE

Now that you have a better understanding of what self-compassion is, let's apply that knowledge by starting some practices.

1. Set a simple intention or vow such as: *I will be kinder and gentler with myself and more supportive and understanding.*

2. Make a list of how you'd like to, or already do, care for yourself. It's helpful to consider these five categories:
   - Physically: How do you soften your body? Exercise, get a massage, take a bath, make a cup of tea, eat a healthy meal or snack, stretch, dance, take a walk or bike ride, nap, practice yoga.
   - Mentally: How do you care for your mind especially when stressed? Watch a funny movie, read an inspiring book or entertaining magazine, sunbathe, listen to music, color, take items off your to-do list, watch the clouds or stars, listen to a guided meditation.
   - Emotionally: How do you soothe and comfort yourself? Get a hug, cuddle your fur baby, read poetry or write a poem, have a good cry (watching an emotional movie helps), talk to a good friend, coach, or therapist, journal, garden, play, cook something healthy and delicious.

- Relationally: How do you connect with others in ways that feel good? Hang out with friends, play a game, give someone you love a call, edit your social media feed to get negative people out of your life.
- Spiritually: What do you do to care for your soul? Read, meditate, pray, spend time in nature, go to church or temple, practice yoga, take a media fast and unplug (i.e. turn off your cell phone).

3. Forgive yourself. Stop beating yourself up and punishing yourself when you make a mistake or fail. Remember common humanity—we are all imperfect and make mistakes. Be gentle with yourself. Learn from past mistakes and then let them go. Give yourself time and space to grow.

4. Make peace with your inner critic. When she or your perfectionist pop up, thank them for trying to help you. Then turn on your self-compassionate voice by talking to yourself the way you would a good friend. (In the Appendix, I have provided resources that can support your self-compassion practice.)

Start where you are, and focus on progress, not perfection. There's actually no such thing as perfection with self-compassion. Accept yourself right now exactly as you are.

Congratulations, you've started your self-love *JOurneY*. No worries if you get lost along the way. It's all part of the self-love trip. I'm here to help. If you have questions or need direction, please join my supportive Facebook community of women who are loving themselves and rocking midlife: Dr Ellen's Mastermind[5]. I'd love to hear how your self-love adventure is going.

Feeling energized? You should be! Loving, rather than loathing yourself, liberates and generates a tremendous amount of energy.

Now get ready to take your vibe even higher with Step 3: Energize Yourself.

CHAPTER SUMMARY:

- Depression is common at midlife. If you have overwhelming feelings of sadness, loneliness, and depression that last for a long period of time, get professional, medical help.
- Self-criticism is the internalized voice of early caregivers. It's trying to keep you safe but is causing more harm than good. Shine a light on your self-critic.
- *Wabi-sabi* your life. See and appreciate the beauty that is imperfect, impermanent, and incomplete.
- Practice self-compassion by treating yourself like a good friend. Be kind to yourself and mindful when you notice you are struggling. Remember, we all make mistakes and are imperfect beings.

5

STEP #3: ENERGIZE YOURSELF: FROM POOPED TO SUPERCHARGED

*Even though the body appears to be material, it is not.
In the deeper reality, your body is a field of energy,
transformation and intelligence.*

— Deepak Chopra

A decade ago my energy was so low that I felt like I needed to run an IV from the coffee machine to my brachial artery in order to get moving. Physically, mentally, emotionally, and spiritually exhausted, I fit the bill for burnout, a condition now recognized by the World Health Organization as an occupational phenomenon and medical condition. Completely drained by difficult relationships and a negative, stressful environment, I had to dip deep into my depleted adrenal reserves to do my job as a personal fitness trainer.

To compound matters, I had undiagnosed Hashimoto's disease. An autoimmune disorder that destroys the thyroid gland, Hashimoto's is the leading cause of thyroid disorders for midlife women. Without a properly functioning thyroid gland regulating my metabolism, I felt like crap.

Rather than slowing down, I fueled myself with caffeine and gluten-heavy carbs, which further eroded my thyroid. If you have a genetic predisposition to Hashimoto's, eating gluten can turn on the switch that triggers your immune system to attack the thyroid. Like a junkie, I'd pop Penguin Caffeinated Mints and carry a travel mug filled with coffee just to function. No one knew. Jumping around on the gym floor and inspiring others during group exercise classes, I hid my exhaustion well, even from myself.

Fast forward a decade, I've slowed down yet accomplish more and feel uber energized. I have my health back thanks to a more life-friendly lifestyle and a daily dose of Levothyroxine, a synthetic thyroid hormone. I officially entered menopause a couple of years ago, so the draining side effects of that transition, like hot flashes and insomnia, are behind me.

What's my superpower to be supercharged? It starts with self-love and self-compassion. As you learned in the last chapter, self-love fosters the courage to stop doing things that insult your soul. This creates space for healthier, heart-centered behaviors and thoughts to emerge. When you do more of what is aligned with rather than insults your soul, your vibration is higher and you have much more energy. Rather than fighting life, you're in the flow. Supported by a Law of Attraction (like attracts like) sloop, you experience smooth sailing.

For a long time, I was *in irons,* a sailing term for not moving because you're heading into the wind. What got me moving forward was changing course and navigating via the music in my heart. Not only did I change direction, but I also healed and released a lot—a toxic marriage, perfectionism, people-pleasing, and layers of fear— fear of being myself, listening to my inner wisdom, and shining brightly. Acceptance has helped me to let go of the need to control everything in my life. I've developed the faith that everything is working for my highest good. You'll learn exactly how to do this in Step 5: Empower Yourself, but first, you need some energetic wind in your sails.

I'm living in a whole new energetic vibe. Midlife crisis? No way. I'm experiencing a midlife oasis. I wake up energized, joyful, and excited to start my day, and you can too.

The key is learning how to manage your energy and raise your vibe so you can thrive. Even in crazy, chaotic times, you can use simple, powerful tools and techniques to go from pooped to supercharged.

In this chapter, I'm going to show you exactly how to elevate your vibe so you have the energy to transform your life because if you're exhausted, you're more likely to sit on the couch and watch Netflix than take action.

WHAT'S DRAINING YOU?

Before we discuss getting supercharged, let's look at what might be compromising your energy level. Once you know what your energy leaks are, you can plug them so you generate more juice.

In your 7-Day Plan for Action in Part III, I've provided a simple, powerful exercise that involves keeping track of all the activities in your day and rating them according to how energizing or draining they make you feel. You also rate whether or not you experience *flow*—the state where you lose track of time because you are challenged and enjoying what you're doing.

Midlife fatigue is as common as creaky knees, gray hair, and wrinkles. Perimenopausal hormone fluctuations can also negatively impact your energy levels. A study published in the *Journal of the American Geriatrics Society* found that nearly a third of adults age fifty-one and older experience fatigue.

Riding the waves of midlife can leave you dizzy and exhausted. You may feel sandwiched between caring for kids, aging parents, and a needy spouse who seems like he can barely tie his shoes.

There's so much to do and so many people to care for that your plate can become too full, especially if you've forgotten how to say no to others and yes to yourself. Trying to please others is draining and leaves little time to relax and recharge. You simply can't pour from an empty cup.

In addition, we live in a toxic "hustle" culture that glamorizes workaholism and pressures us to work all the time. The hustle culture became epidemic during the pandemic because everyone worked from home. There was no escaping the office. It was in your face and in the kitchen, bedroom, and living room. Many of my clients worked from 6 a.m. to 8 p.m. and were available for their clients or team 24/7.

Self-care is a postscript, and the more you work, the better person you are.

Spending ten to fourteen hours a day sitting in Zoom meetings, missing meals, and skipping the gym is lauded. Rather than encouraging teamwork and wellness, the culture promotes competition and burnout. However, ignoring basic physiological signals like hunger and fatigue results in dis-ease.

For midlife women trying to keep their jobs and not become redundant, this hustle culture is particularly stressful and noxious. There's always a millennial who wants your job and has more energy and few if any caretaker responsibilities.

The hectic lifestyle has a cost—exhaustion and frustration, which ironically undermine performance. Like an elite athlete, if you want peak performance, you have to build rest and self-care into your training schedule.

Despite what your work culture may encourage, you can slow down a little. Take responsibility for your life and the need to go ninety miles an hour. You are a human *being,* not a human *doing.* You have control over your calendar, so unschedule yourself and simplify your life. Many of my clients find that they can designate responsibility to others, opt-out or say no more often, and only attend meetings that matter.

Start by taking a few minutes in the morning to set the tone for your day. A brisk ten-minute walk or few minutes contemplating the day can make a huge difference in how you feel and function.

Schedule breaks to eat and move your body. Hold walking meetings. Your co-workers will appreciate this too. I know this is difficult, particularly because our culture praises doing over being, but you actually will be more productive and have more energy if you take your time and take care of yourself. And multitasking, which we'll discuss in the next chapter—forget about it. Research shows it makes you less effective.

MEDICAL CONDITIONS THAT CAUSE FATIGUE

If you're tired most of the time, there may be an underlying medical condition that needs to be investigated and addressed. I've already mentioned thyroid issues, which are a leading cause of fatigue, especially in women. One in eight women will develop a thyroid issue in her lifetime. Other medical conditions that can cause fatigue are anemia, heart disease, insomnia, certain medications, and mental health challenges.

Anemia, which happens when you don't have enough healthy red blood cells, is common in perimenopausal women because of excessive blood loss during menstruation. Often undiagnosed, it can cause many of the symptoms associated with perimenopause, including fatigue, headaches, and brain fog. Anemia can be due to excessive bleeding; certain medications; and low levels of iron, B12, or folic acid. Since treatment depends on the cause, talk with your doctor and get a blood test so you can determine the best approach to fix it.

Heart disease, which is the leading cause of death in women, can also result in fatigue. According to the Centers for Disease Control and Prevention (CDC), the number of women between the ages of forty-four and sixty-five dying from heart disease is increasing. When your heart isn't working properly, your cells don't receive adequate oxygen, and you feel tired. Lifestyle changes, which I'll elaborate on in this chapter, including eating a healthier diet, regular exercise, managing stress, and quitting smoking if you're a smoker, can help reverse heart disease.

Sleep issues, which impact over a third of Americans, according to the National Sleep Foundation, can leave you feeling tired during the day too. Fortunately, there are a number of things you can do to improve the quality of your sleep, which I'll explain later in this chapter.

Now that we've addressed what might be sapping your energy, let's look at how you can raise your vibe and increase your energy.

WHAT IS YOUR ENERGETIC VIBRATION?

In your elementary school science class, you may have learned that energy is the ability to do work, and that there are two kinds of energy: kinetic or moving energy, and potential or stored energy. What your fifth-grade science teacher probably didn't mention is that you, and absolutely everything in the universe, from the chair you are sitting on to OGLE-2014-BLG-0124L (the most distant planet astronomers have discovered), is energy.

Einstein was right: $E = mc^2$—energy equals mass times the speed of light squared. Drill down to the quantum or subatomic level, and you'll see that energy and mass (matter) are interchangeable. While this isn't what we perceive, energy can become mass and mass can become energy. Matter isn't

> *Everything in life is vibration*
>
> —Albert Einstein

solid. Rather it consists of both waves and particles. These seemingly solid particles are actually vibrating like waves rippling across the ocean.

Yes, it's confusing and not intuitive. As Danish physicist and Nobel Prize winner Niels Bohr is quoted as saying, "If you can think about quantum theory without getting dizzy, you don't get it." Don't worry if you don't understand it. No one knows exactly how quantum theory works. After all, it's a theory—scientists' best idea based on evidence about how the subatomic world works.

While you may feel as solid as this book that you're reading (unless, of course, it's digital), you are a living energy field. Your body is made of parts—cells, organs, and tissues—all vibrating at different rates and producing various frequencies of energy. Nonphysical aspects of you, such as your chakras (invisible spinning energy disks that radiate from the base of your spine to the top of your head) and aura (an invisible energy force that surrounds you) also vibrate at specific frequencies. Your vibration is the totality of all your energy.

There are many ways to classify vibrations, which are a kind of rhythm. For example, we can look to our five senses to detect the vibration of sound, sight, taste, smell, and touch. In my holistic coaching work, I like to categorize energy as physical, mental, emotional, spiritual, and relational. These are the areas that I feel midlife women need to work on the most to achieve balance and wellness and raise their vibe.

Still not convinced that you are energy and that energy and matter are interchangeable? Consider the fact that you are literally made of sunlight. The cells in your body come from the food you eat, which in turn either comes from plants that are fueled by sunlight or animals that eat plants.

On a more complex level, if you exploded the cells in your body or any form of matter, you would see that 99 percent of what appears solid is actually empty space. Every human is made of millions and millions of atoms, which are mostly empty space.

HOW TO RAISE YOUR VIBE

What's exciting is that you can influence your energetic vibration to optimize happiness, health, and wellbeing. You can do this by working on your body, mind, heart, spirit, and relationships. By raising your vibe in these areas, you can elevate your mood, become healthier, and boost your ability to reach your goals and intentions.

To help determine what to shift, first take my Raise Your Vibe Quiz[6]. When you make these shifts, your life will change dramatically and start to move in a more positive, empowered direction.

As you raise your vibe, keep two things in mind. First, as you learned in the last chapter, always make changes from a place of self-love rather than self-loathing. This is key because when you work on yourself from a place of self-loathing, focusing on changing what you don't want rather than moving towards what you do want, you drag what's wrong with you into your future reality, and then that's what keeps showing up. Second, be patient. It takes time for your external reality to match up with the internal, energetic shifts that you are making. Morphing into a butterfly seems to happen magically, but transformation takes time and work. Like a caterpillar, you have to digest what's not working as you lay down your blueprint for what's next.

"Here is the amazing thing," says biologist Bruce Lipton on his website, "The caterpillar and the butterfly have the exact same DNA. They are the same organism but are receiving and responding to different organizing signals." You're the same person in terms of the information coded in your being, but you are awakening to new possibilities based on your new energy.

Accept where you're at and trust the process. If you are following your heart and doing what's right for you, everything will work out for your highest good. Affirm it!

Okay, let's get started on supercharging your life and elevating your vibe.

HIGH PERFORMANCE PYRAMID

One framework I love for energizing your life is the High Performance Pyramid. Developed by Jim Loehr and Tony Schwartz, it is a holistic model that helps people maximize their capacities on four levels of a pyramid: physical, emotional, mental, and spiritual. High energy comes from achieving the ideal performance state (IPS). This happens when all four levels of the pyramid are in sync and working together over the long term, even under stress and pressure. (In this chapter, I'll cover how to rock your physical energy. In the next chapter, you'll learn how to better manage your mental energy. I'll cover managing emotional, relational, and finally spiritual energy in Chapters 7, 8, and 9.)

According to Schwartz and Loehr, authors of *The Power of Full Engagement: Managing Energy, Not Time, Is the Key to High Performance and Personal Renewal,* "Every one of our thoughts, emotions, and behaviors has an energy consequence. The ultimate measure of our lives is not how much time we spend on the planet, but rather how much energy we invest in the time that we have."

The key to achieving IPS is using daily rituals to recover energy when you spend it. Regular rituals keep you energized and link the levels of the pyramid together.

As Loehr and Schwartz explain, managing your energy has two key components: "oscillation," which they define as movement between energy expenditure (stress) and energy renewal (recovery) and regular rituals that promote oscillation.

Think about the levels as energy buckets that need to be filled on a daily basis. Just like you need to refuel your car, you've got to fill up to ensure that you make it to your destination, the next chapter. Not only will keeping your tanks full improve your performance, but it will also keep you motivated, passionate, and enthusiastic about your projects so you can achieve your goals and dreams.

Throw out the idea that you've got to go through pain to be successful. While the, "I can do anything I set my mind to attitude" is great, the belief that "strength comes from struggle" leads to burnout. I've been there, and when the caffeine/sugar buzz stops working, you have to find a better way to run your body and life. Keep it fueled with high-octane food, move it daily, get adequate rest, and your body will reward you with energy, radiance, and balance. Conversely, feed it low-octane fuel, stay sedentary, and rob it of rest, and you'll become depleted, out of balance, and prone to dis-ease.

Simple Ways to Fill Your Tank

When you notice your energy is low, rather than plowing forward, stop and refill your empty tank. Notice which bucket is most in need of replenishing and then pick a quick activity. Here are easy things you can do to fill yourself up when you are depleted and need an energy infusion.

Mental moves to feel light rather than edgy and irritable:
- Meditate: Use a guided meditation, focus on your breath, or repeat a mantra.
- Visualize your happy place, such as the beach, mountains, or forest.
- Take a shower. Bonus points when you shift the temp from hot to cool.

Physical activities to invigorate you:
- Brisk walk + sunshine + fresh air = energized you.
- Take a ten- to twenty-minute nap.
- Hydrate and have a healthy snack.

Emotional shifts to feel calmer and more positive:

- Depending on your desired mood, listen to upbeat or relaxing music.
- Read inspirational quotes.
- Call a friend.

Spiritual activities to elevate your consciousness:

- Journal.
- Be kind to or help someone else out.
- Read an inspiring biography.

FUELING UP: LET'S TALK NUTRITION

I've been a registered dietitian since 1993 and have seen diet fads come and go. Actually the same regimes and schemes are usually just re-spun and renamed. For example, the low carb, high protein diet has been around since 776 BC when the Greek Olympic athletes ate a meat-heavy, high protein low carb diet. Fast forward to the 1950s, and we had The Cabbage Soup Diet and Eat Fat & Grow Slim. Next, there was Stillman, followed by Atkins and Scarsdale. The new millennium brought us South Beach and Keto.

In my nearly three decades of sharing eating regimes, I've found that one diet does it all: Whole Foods Plant-Based - WFPB for short.

While there are numerous opinions around which diet is best, reams of research show that plant-based diets can also lower your risk of heart disease, hypertension, diabetes, digestive disease, colon cancer, and breast cancer. Eating the WFPB way can also help reduce your cholesterol level and prevent menopausal weight gain. In addition, eating more fiber (the part of plant foods we don't digest) helps stabilize estrogen levels, which can reduce the number of hot flashes and night sweats you experience.

If this diet is so amazing, why don't we eat this way? Strip away the processing and packaging, and subtract the hard to pronounce artificial ingredients, and the food industry is out-of-business. There's not much money to be made selling kale, carrots, brown rice, and chickpeas. To keep us hooked on SAD (Standard American Diet) and hijack our taste buds, the food industry heavily processes food, dosing it with chemicals and plenty of fat, salt, and sugar. Not only are these ingredients cheap, they condition your brain's reward center to crave more and more. Try to eat one potato chip or one M & M. It's almost impossible.

Plus we've been taught to view food in terms of *macronutrients* (carbs, protein, and fats), *micronutrients* (vitamins and minerals), and total *calories.* As a registered dietitian, I learned to quantify food using this rubric. It provided an easy way to determine certain qualities of an individual's diet, mainly grams of fat, protein, and carbohydrates, and total calories.

There was no discussion about the energetic frequency or vibe of food. Food, like everything in the universe, has vibrational properties. Every time you eat, you absorb the food's energy into your body.

Natural, whole foods, particularly raw and organic plants, are packed with energy from the sun. That energy is vibrating at a high frequency. When you eat these plants, your body, mind, emotions, and spirit benefit.

Highly processed foods, especially those with hard to pronounce chemical ingredients that your grandmother would not have recognized (like butylated hydroxytoluene, BHT for short, an ingredient commonly added to gum and margarine that some studies show causes cancer in rodents) have had the natural energy stripped away. Designed to maximize shelf-life, not human life, they are low vibe.

Think fresh strawberries versus strawberry Twizzlers, or Tang versus fresh-squeezed orange juice. If a food rots quickly, it has more life force than a food that could remain intact for centuries in a time capsule.

As kids in the sixties and seventies, we midlifers were brainwashed to think that modern, fortified foods in bright, fun packages were better for us than real food that didn't come in a box with a picture of Captain Crunch or Count Chocula on it. I see this attitude in clients all the time who favor eating a granola bar over an apple with a handful of almonds.

The push towards processed food started in the 1940s when the government set rationing points that made these foods easier to obtain. It was margarine over butter. A couple of decades later, even Mother Nature couldn't tell the difference between Chiffon margarine and butter. No one told her the trans fats used to make margarine were clogging her arteries.

In the 1950s, Swanson introduced the frozen turkey dinner giving women a taste for a utopian future where they didn't need to cook. Then we got Tang, invented in 1957 by food scientist William Mitchell at General Foods (who also created Cool Whip, Jell-O, and Pop Rocks) and marketed as an orange juice substitute. Shelf-stable and packed with vitamin C, it became popular after astronaut John Glen drank it while orbiting the earth in the Friendship 7.

Whole plant-based foods, the foods our parents and grandparents grew up on, seemed boring in comparison. However, there's nothing more exciting for your body's cells. Fresh fruits and veggies are filled with *prana*—life force energy—so when you eat them, you receive their vibe and feel energized.

Consider how you'd feel after consuming a slice of pepperoni pizza and soda versus how you'd feel after eating a colorful, fresh salad full of greens, sprouts, and legumes. If you're like most people, you'll feel tired and heavy with the former and light and energized with the latter. That's because the whole food plant-based foods are nourishing your body and giving you energy, while the pizza and soda are creating a toxic load and stress on your system.

When you eat high vibe, whole plant foods, you also automatically eliminate low vibe, health-compromising ingredients such as high-fructose corn syrup, salt, refined grains, hydrogenated oils, sodium phosphate, synthetic dyes, genetically modified organisms (GMOs), nitrates, nitrites, MSG, aspartame, BHA & BHT (which are derived from petroleum), and brominated vegetable oil.

Whole plant foods—vegetables, fruits, whole grains, legumes, nuts, cold-pressed oils, especially fresh and organic, carry a high-vibration that nourishes your body, mind, and soul.

Fresh, whole food plant-based foods are also packed with phytochemicals—substances that prevent disease and improve health. ("phyto" means "plant"). Scientists have identified over 5,000 various types. Carrots alone contain over 100 phytochemicals. Blueberries are one of the richest sources of antioxidant phytochemicals.

While we don't need specific amounts of phytochemicals to prevent nutrient deficiencies, eating a diet high in phytochemicals raises your vibe and protects your cells from free radical damage. Filling up on phytochemicals can also boost your immune system, lower blood pressure, protect your brain from cognitive decline, and help prevent age-related diseases, including diabetes, heart disease, and osteoporosis. Estrogen-like phytochemicals called *flavonoids* found in soybeans, chickpeas, and licorice may help reduce breast cancers that depend on estrogen for growth.

You may have heard the expression: *eat the rainbow*. It's good advice because each plant chemical has a different color and frequency. The different phytochemicals help determine the characteristic color, smell, and flavor of various plant foods. Carotenoids—found in carrots, sweet potatoes, and apricots—give plants their orange color. Anthocyanins give grapes and blueberries their red, purple, and blue hues while providing anti-inflammatory and anti-tumor properties. Less vibrant-looking plant foods including nuts, potatoes, chocolate, tea, and cauliflower also are packed with high-vibe phytonutrients.

WFPB DIET BENEFITS YOUR MICROBIOME

Right now approximately thirty-seven trillion microorganisms—mostly bacteria along with fungi, parasites, and viruses—are living in your body. Collectively known as the *microbiome*, these microbes weigh more than your brain and are almost as vital. A new, exciting field of research is showing that your microbiome shapes your health and influences everything from mood to metabolism.

While you can't see or feel them, they are essential for your survival. In fact, this universe of organisms in your gut is so important that the microbiome is often referred to as a "forgotten organ." When you're healthy, your microbiome works symbiotically with your body supporting the immune system, metabolism, and circadian rhythms; fostering good mental health; reducing disease risk, and even aiding weight loss.

Research has shown that the microbiome plays a key role in conditions such as asthma and allergies, and in several autoimmune diseases including diabetes, muscular dystrophy, rheumatoid arthritis, fibromyalgia, and multiple sclerosis.

There are thousands of different species of microorganisms living inside your body and on the surface of your skin. Your individual bacterial community is established during birth and through breast milk. Unique as your fingerprint, it changes across your lifetime. Diet, overall health, environment, and illness all influence it. Overuse of antibiotics and a refined diet can cause a condition called *dysbiosis,* where pathogenic and symbiotic microbes become unbalanced, undermining health.

While more research is needed, it is becoming clear that a healthy gut can help create a healthy mind. A new field of study called *nutritional psychiatry* is evolving to help understand how gut health and diet can have a positive or negative impact on mood. The potential to boost mood and treat conditions including anxiety, depression, and Alzheimer's disease by altering the composition of the microbiome is huge. In fact, it's so promising that scientists have even started to experiment with fecal transplants to better understand how different compositions of gut flora impact health and disease.

Whole plant-based foods contain lots of prebiotics, which are indigestible carbohydrate compounds. Prebiotic foods, which are mostly fiber, pass through your body and feed your good bacteria, keeping your microbiome healthy.

Prebiotics are found in a variety of plant foods from fruits and vegetables to beans, seeds, and grains. Good choices include garlic, onions, leeks, asparagus, apples, bananas, legumes, tomatoes, soybeans, flaxseed, chicory root, barley, and oats. Other foods that help create a healthier microbiome include fermented foods such as yogurt, kefir, sauerkraut, and kombucha. Research shows that drinking tea may also promote a well-balanced gut. Reducing stress and sleeping well can also have a positive impact on the microbiome.

If you really want to support your microbiome, consider swapping chemically-laden home cleaning products for gentler, more natural products. Yes, the chemical ones may kill 99 percent of germs, but they also kill healthy bacteria that your body picks up from your environment.

Ditto on the chemically-laden personal care products. Your skin and scalp are covered with bacteria, so keep them healthy by using natural products rather than the traditional antibacterial deodorants and antiperspirants, and chemical shampoos and conditioners.

Here are two more moves that will improve your gut health *and* raise your vibe: play with your dog and dig in the dirt. Both can introduce more diversity of microorganisms in your gut. An increasing amount of research shows that exposure to plants, particularly in gardening, benefits mental and physical health. Spending time with pets raises the highest vibe—love.

SAVE THE PLANET AND WHITTLE YOUR WAISTLINE

Need more reasons to eat the whole food plant-based way? Besides being environmentally friendly (growing plant foods uses fewer resources than foods of animal origin), whole food plant-based diets are typically lower in calories than the Standard American Diet (SAD). Plant foods contain water and fiber, so they fill you up without filling you out. You feel content while consuming fewer calories, so you eat less. The only exceptions are nuts and seeds. While they are healthy, you have to consider portion sizes because these foods are high in fat and calories. A small handful, about an ounce and a half, is considered a healthy serving.

The only downside to the WFPB lifestyle is that it requires you to change your eating and shopping habits. Yes, it can also be more expensive to eat this way, but what is your health and feeling energized worth to you?

Eating a whole foods plant-based diet doesn't mean that you have to go full-on vegan and completely eliminate meat, poultry, fish, eggs, and dairy. You can still eat foods of animal origin, just reduce the amount of processed foods and animal products that you eat, and increase the amount of whole food plant-based products. When you do purchase meat, fish, poultry, or dairy, try to buy organic or sustainable, humanely sourced products.

It's helpful to consider not making meat the center of your plate. Think of it as a complement, not the focal point. Look to ethnic cuisines that use small amounts of meat as a condiment to flavor soups, stews, casseroles, and stir-fries. Perhaps go meatless one day or meal a week, or sub out a category of animal products. For example, replace beef with veggie burgers and plant-based "ground round," or scrambled eggs with tofu.

The Special Nutritional Needs of Midlife Women

After fifty, women have higher protein requirements: 1 to 1.5 grams per kilogram (one kilogram = 2.2. pounds) of body weight compared to 0.8 for the general adult population. This means that if you weigh 150 pounds, you need between 68 and 102 grams of protein a day. Adequate protein is important because it helps to prevent the loss of muscle mass, which is a natural part of the aging process.

Healthy sources of animal protein include fish, chicken, low-fat dairy products, lean meats, and eggs. Good vegetarian protein sources include beans, soy foods, nuts, seeds, and some whole grains.

To promote bone health and prevent osteoporosis, women over fifty also need more calcium, about 1,200 mgs a day, compared to younger women who only have an RDA of 1,000 mgs.

It's also important to get adequate vitamin D to support calcium absorption. Sunlight is the natural source of vitamin D, but many people don't get enough, especially people who live in the north. The US Institute of Medicine recommends an average daily intake of 400-800 IU, but some studies recommended higher levels of 1000-4000 IU, the safe upper limit.

While I'm not 100 percent vegan, I eat the WFPB most of the time. I love eating this way. Plant foods taste great and are an integral part of me living a long, high vibe life. By eating frequent meals that contain lots of plants and fiber, I don't experience blood sugar spikes and cravings for coffee, chocolate, and sugary snacks.

Here's what my typical day of eating looks like. I start my day with a large glass of water and a cup of green tea. An hour or so later I have a slice of gluten-free, whole grain bread with peanut butter and a green smoothie that typically contains half a banana, berries, a large handful of greens, soy-based protein powder, and some vibe-enhancing extras like wheatgrass powder or goji berries. Lunch is usually a huge salad that contains a wide array of vegetables and tofu, beans, or canned fish. In the summer, I go right out to the garden and pick whatever is fresh. For dinner, I often have a veggie burger and cut up veggies with hummus.

I also drink plenty of filtered water throughout the day. The recommendation is roughly half your body weight in ounces of water. This means if you weigh 150 pounds you should drink about seventy-five ounces of water daily.

I've cut way down on the amount of grain products I eat. I find it helps me feel more energized, reduces inflammation especially in my joints, and keeps me at a healthy weight.

Dieting—Just Say NO!

Whether you've been on one or a million diets, tried everything from Atkins to the Zone, just say no to dieting. Diets are temporary measures that promise the world but don't deliver.

Ironically, the research shows that diets predict weight gain, not loss. Diets fail for numerous reasons. First, they are temporary, "quick-fix" solutions to a long-term, societal issue. The problem is that we live in an *obesogenic* environment—one that promotes eating more and moving less.

Dieting feeds obesity. Calorie deprivation lowers metabolism, so you burn fewer calories. It also promotes hunger and increases stress, which triggers overeating. Diets also teach you to ignore your body's natural signals—the exact signals you need to heed to reach and maintain a healthy weight. The only entity that benefits from dieting is the diet industry. They want you to fail so you'll buy their magic bullet solutions again and again.

Throw out the diet books and trash the weight loss apps along with the guilt for not taking better care of yourself in the past. It's okay. Ditch the punitive approach and self-flagellation. It generates cortisol, which erodes your energy and motivation. A better approach is to take care of yourself because you want to feel good and have energy to make your next chapter your best chapter.

Start by making Project Energize Yourself part of your self-love journey, and everything will flow from there. Not only is restrictive eating no fun but it's also not sustainable. Transforming your energy levels and body at midlife is challenging enough. You don't need your self-critic on your back trying to pummel off the pounds.

TRANSFORMING BODY IMAGE

I used to think that when my body was perfect my body image would improve. So I counted every calorie and worked out like a fiend getting absolutely nowhere on that damn spin bike. I was always chasing a media-created image of perfection, and sweating my ass off wasn't getting me closer to that ideal. The ideal only exists on Instagram and in the pages of glossy women's magazines. The media shows us images of perfection on purpose. They want us to feel bad about our bodies, so we'll buy the products and services that they are hawking.

My personal fitness clients felt the same way. In contrast, many of my male clients could be fifty pounds overweight and look seven months pregnant and yet perceive themselves as sexy stallions.

I remember conversations with one of my favorite regulars, Tracy. Tracy was an accomplished professional, grandmother, and world traveler. She was in amazing shape able to climb Machu Picchu and go on hundred-mile bike treks. Despite all she had achieved, not a workout session went by without her pinching her belly and saying: "I hate my body. This flab just won't go away. I can't stand it. Let's do more ab work today."

Planks, sit-ups, cardio… no matter what we did, nothing melted it and her bad body image. Even though her slightly soft flesh was normal—a side effect of two pregnancies—she was considering plastic surgery. Retrospectively, I wish I knew what I know now: practice self-compassion. It will help you feel better about your body and yourself.

Here's the thing, negative body image—how you perceive your body—is in your head, not your body. You can feel good about your body right now exactly as it is, not when you lose ten pounds or have washboard abs.

As I discussed in the last chapter, if you're struggling with negative body image, keep practicing self-compassion. Self-compassion will seriously transform your body image because, when you love yourself, you stop judging every jiggle and wrinkle. When you care about your wellbeing, you go on that daily walk, get to bed on time, and make an effort to eat right.

If you're like most midlife women, you've probably spent a lot of time taking your body for granted and/or actively criticizing it. Despite how you treat your body, it continues to serve you year after year.

ROCK YOUR MIDLIFE LAB
Appreciate your body

Now it's your opportunity to appreciate your body. To do so, simply take a few minutes to answer the question: What has my body done for me? And then grab your journal or *Rock Your Midlife Playbook*[i] and write down your answers. Make a list stating all the wonderful ways your body serves you. It's a very powerful way to improve both your relationship with your body and increase your overall wellbeing.

Starting today, look in the mirror and complement your body. Thank your trillions of cells for keeping you alive. You may feel silly, but know that sending your body positive thoughts promotes wellness. Feeling good about your body will also motivate you to take that yoga class and have an apple instead of a candy bar for a snack.

MOVE TO RAISE YOUR VIBE

Along with fuel, two key factors that influence your physical vibe are movement and rest. Think you need to go the *no pain, no gain* route when it comes to fitness? Consider how the punishing workouts leave you feeling. Take your cue from elite athletes who know the importance of rest days. Less is really more at midlife. We can do hard things, but we also have to be gentler on our aging bodies because recovery takes longer than it did in our twenties and thirties.

Decades of research show that the key to increasing physical strength and maintaining or perhaps even building muscle mass, which is so important at midlife, is rest. When you lift weights you create small tears in muscle fibers. Muscles adapt by becoming stronger, but they need time to heal. The National Strength and Conditioning Association (NSC) recommends 48-72 hours of recovery time between weight training workouts. If you stress them without giving them a chance to recover you may injure yourself.

The biggest issue I find with fitness for women at midlife is finding the time to fit movement into your schedule. The truth is it's not about finding the time but making the time. You have to prioritize fitness by making a date with yourself to exercise and establish a regular routine.

Here are six tips to make exercise happen:

1. Put the time you are going to exercise in your calendar with an alarm.

2. Start small. For example, set a goal to walk three times a

week for 15 minutes, rather than seven times a week for 30.

3. Pack your gym bag or lay out your exercise gear ahead of time.
4. Do an activity you enjoy. To increase the pleasure factor, link it with another activity such as walking with a good friend or listening to an audiobook.
5. Reward yourself when you reach your goal.
6. Get support and create clear work-life boundaries. Ask your family and co-workers to be cheerleaders. Find accountability partners who will make sure that you fit in a time for a walk or exercise class.

Try to integrate all three elements of fitness—cardio, strength training, and stretching—into your exercise routine. Cardio reduces stress and exercises the heart, and will help you reach and maintain a healthy weight. Strength training will enable you to continue everyday activities of life and prevent muscle mass from declining. Stretching helps reduce aches and pains and increases your mobility and range of motion.

If you're new to exercising regularly, be patient in terms of feeling good. It may take a few weeks before you notice that working out increases your energy and vibe and reduces stress. Exercise is nature's Prozac, so you'll start to notice that your mind, not just your body, feels better. Not only will you feel more joyful, vital, and youthful, you'll accomplish more because you have more energy and focus.

REST AND SLEEP

To keep your vibe high, it's also important to rest. Taking a ten-to-twenty-minute nap when you're dragging will do a lot more for your energy level than reaching for caffeine and sugar.

Power naps have numerous benefits. They can help reduce sleepiness and stress, aid memory and learning, and regulate your emotions. A study published in the *British Medical Journal* found that a short nap once or twice a week may even lower your risk of heart attack or stroke.

It's important that your nap is the right length. Under ten minutes and you won't get enough rest for it to help. Napping for more than thirty minutes can leave you feeling groggy rather than supercharged and may interfere with nighttime sleep.

There are a number of things you can do to nap successfully. Schedule your nap between one and three o'clock, after lunch when energy levels naturally dip. Find a comfortable, quiet place where you won't be disturbed. You may want to use an eye cover and headphones to block noise. If you work in an office and there's no place to nap, consider using your car. Set a timer so you nap between ten and twenty minutes.

Sleep can be a problem during midlife. According to the Sleep Foundation, sleep issues affect 39 to 47 percent of perimenopausal women and 35 to 60 percent of postmenopausal women. Work pressure and caregiver responsibilities can keep you up at night. Fluctuating hormone levels during perimenopause can trigger mental health challenges like anxiety and mood swings, and night sweats and hot flashes, all of which can disturb sleep. Loss of sleep can make you even more anxious, irritable, and stressed, and lower your vibe.

There are a number of things you can do to improve your sleep. First, create a bedtime routine. Go to bed at the same time each night, early enough to allow you to get seven to eight hours of rest. Turn off all screens (TV, phone, and computer) at least an hour prior to bed. Stimulating media and blue light from screens can interfere with proper sleep. To relax sip chamomile tea, listen to soothing music, read, or meditate. Avoid caffeine in the afternoon and cut down on alcohol, which can interfere with normal sleep. Eat an early, light dinner. Make sure your bedroom is dark, quiet, and cool. Exercising regularly and letting worry go can also help.

Night sweats or hot flashes disrupting your sleep? Take the diet advice I shared to heart, and eat more soy foods. They contain phytoestrogens that studies suggest help balance hormone levels. Wear light, cotton sleepwear or sleep naked. Keep your room temperature low and a fan by your bed. In a spray bottle, mix a few drops of lemon juice with cool water and spritz on yourself when you're hot. Avoid potential triggers including caffeine, smoking, alcohol, and spicy food. Maintaining a healthy weight, exercising regularly, and reducing stress can also help.

You may also want to consider supplemental *melatonin*, a hormone naturally made by the pineal gland that declines with age and helps regulate sleep-wake cycles. An overview in the scientific journal *Sleep Science* discussing the link between sleep, melatonin, and the menopausal transition concluded that, "difficulties with falling asleep can be reliably alleviated by low doses of melatonin. While more research is needed, the data suggest that women treated with melatonin also experience considerable improvement in mood disturbances and depression." In addition, a meta-analysis published in the *International Journal of Endocrinology* concluded that, "melatonin might be used as a safe nutritional supplement to improve bone density in perimenopausal and postmenopausal women."

SOME FINAL THOUGHTS TO GET YOU
ON THE HIGH-VIBE PATH

As you start to supercharge your physical energy, please discard the old ways of going about lifestyle change. Forget the crash diets and punishing trips to the gym and the idea that you will finally love your body and yourself when you have a "perfect" physique.

Start where you are. Take a fresh look at your lifestyle and make a few changes every week. Move a little more and sit a little less. The more active you are, the better you'll feel and the more energy you'll have. Prioritize sleep and rest. Schedule exercise and downtime. Examine your diet. What changes would feel expansive—eating more fruits and veggies? Planning and preparing healthy meals? Decluttering your pantry and throwing out foods that are sapping your energy?

Yes, at midlife you may have less energy than you did in your twenties and thirties and more responsibilities. However, you're also wiser and have a broader perspective. No matter where you are at today, if you're not happy with your energy level, take action.

Let go of the thoughts about what midlife is supposed to feel like. You might not be dancing as fast as you once did, but you can still feel amazing. Keep your thoughts positive, which brings us to the next step to rock your midlife, Step 4: Reprogram Your Brain!

CHAPTER SUMMARY:

- Like an elite athlete, if you want to experience peak performance you have to build rest and self-care into your schedule.
- Many medical conditions can cause fatigue. If you're tired most of the time, there may be an underlying medical condition that needs to be investigated and addressed, so talk with your physician.
- Your body is a living energy field. You can influence your energetic vibration to optimize happiness, health, and wellbeing by working on your body, mind, heart, spirit, and relationships.
- Women at midlife have higher requirements for some nutrients, including protein and calcium. The one diet that does it all is Whole Foods Plant-Based.
- Moving your body has numerous benefits. Exercise daily because it feels good and is great for you.

6

STEP #4: REPROGRAM YOUR BRAIN: FROM MUDDY WATERS TO A CRYSTAL SPRING

We speak about losing our minds as if it is a bad thing.
I say, lose your mind. Do it purposefully. Find out
who you really are beyond your thoughts and beliefs.
Lose your mind, find your soul.

— Vironika Tugaleva, author, poet,
spoken word artist, life coach

One of the most daunting midlife challenges I faced was mental meltdown. Menopausal brain fog scrambled my gray matter. I was forgetful, overwhelmed, unfocused, stressed, and anxious. All of which left me wondering: Am I losing my mind? Or worse, Is this Alzheimer's?

My brain has always been powerful, able to speed through coursework like a sports car, earning me a bachelor's in economics, a master's in nutrition, and a doctorate in psychology.

But suddenly I felt like a lemon without a repair shop in sight to fix my flat cognition. I could deal with wrinkles, belly flab, and declining hormone levels thanks to Oil of Olay, Planet Fitness, and Levothyroxine, but there was no cream, exercise, or pill to reverse my diminishing brainpower and lack of clarity and positivity.

Perhaps my mind was too full of old information (like the Krebs cycle, the complex series of steps used by aerobic organisms to release stored energy that I force-fed myself twenty-five years ago to pass NUTR 532 and never used again!) to cram in anything new.

Or maybe my brain was eroding with age spiked by too many Cosmos in my twenties and Pinot in my thirties that compromised recall and focus. All I knew was the former laser-sharp, Porsche-of-a-mind felt like a beat-up Yugo.

Full disclosure: I've always been smart and a little ditzy and disorganized. I've baked cookies and forgotten the flour. Searched for my glasses when they were on top of my head. I talk to my dog in a baby voice, frequently dance like no one is watching, and belt out rock ballads or show tunes when I feel like it.

But this was scatterbrained squared. First, I kept losing my keys. Then I couldn't find my cellphone. Yes, I tried to call it, but it was dead because I'd forgotten to charge it!

Every month, I'd miss or mess up an important date or two. Once I took my daughter to the doctor on Tuesday when she had a dentist appointment on Wednesday. I overlooked the annual OB/GYN exam in August that I'd booked in December, and missed a client meeting scheduled for 8 a.m. because I thought we were working together at 10.

My son dazzled me with his calculus, but I couldn't remember what a derivative was, let alone solve a quadratic equation even though I'd earned A's in Calc 2 in college.

Without thinking, I put the milk in the freezer instead of the refrigerator, and when I went to the grocery store to buy more milk, I couldn't remember what I was there for.

The worst part of the midlife cognition dip was forgetting names. I could recall faces and literally see the image of the person I was thinking about, but names? Forget about it.

It became embarrassing, bordering on cringe-worthy.

About a year after leaving my ex, I attended a fifth birthday party for Sangha, a local yoga studio, taking place at Arts Riot, a hip bar, restaurant, and nightclub. The venue was packed and rockin'. I sipped hard cider and danced to Josh Panda, a pumped performer with a four-octave range and chameleon-like ability to adapt to any vocal style or genre.

As Panda started playing "Got To Get You Into My Life," I spotted an old friend, the cofounder of my old neighborhood book group who lived two doors down from my previous residence. Walking my Portuguese Water Dog, Sizzle, I'd run into her several times a week, usually by the mailboxes where we'd chat and catch up. I had been to her home many times and participated in the meal train created to support her after double knee replacement surgery.

Now, here I was on the dance floor clueless, hesitant to say hello to "what's her name" but longing to connect because I hadn't seen her in over a year. I remembered her husband's name, Mark, and knew her name started with J, but I couldn't remember the remaining letters for the life of me.

Names beginning with J ran through my head—Jane, Judy, Julie, Joy, Jennifer, June, Jessica Jasmine, JayLo? The more I tried, the more stressed I got, and the more J's name became elusive as if my old life was completely illusive.

Then the dreaded moment arrived. J smiled, waved, and walked towards me. Since I was with a friend, I'd have to introduce J... I stumbled asking how she was, introduced my friend, and thank God she introduced herself: "Nice to meet you. I'm Jill."

MIDLIFE MIND: A BLESSING

As novelist Kathleen Glasgow writes in *Girl in Pieces*, "It's all right if you can't remember. Our subconscious is spectacularly agile. Sometimes it knows when to take us away, as a kind of protection."

Looking back at my interaction with Jill and inability to remember many details from my stressful, nearly twenty-five-year marriage, I now see fading memories as a blessing. Like Riley Anderson, the heroine of the movie *Inside Out*, my mind was housekeeping—pruning and blending new information, memories, and emotions with old to help me reprogram, so I could thrive in my new chapter. The old self-concepts kept in place for protection and survival by my ego were dissolving, allowing something new to emerge.

What I now realize is that I've traded aspects of my old identity and a smidgen of my cognitive capacity for something much more valuable—love and wisdom. The intellectual angst and existential crisis of my earlier years, along with a hefty dose of depression, has dissipated. I am calmer and more mindful, compassionate, and optimistic than ever. Like a fine leather sofa or wallet, my mind is softer and smoother. To enhance the process, I'm working on myself, intentionally cultivating emotional stability and positivity, fostering new neural connections that conduct waves of peace, happiness, and joy.

And I'm not alone. This new mindset is one of the many blessings of midlife. Studies have shown that individuals ripen with age in a good way. We become mellower and less neurotic, better able to weather emotional hurricanes, leaving us more tranquil and better able to navigate our world.

If you've been experiencing a dip in your mental abilities, rest assured. You're not losing it and don't need to make an appointment with a neurologist. Forgetting where you put your keys, glasses, or cellphone, or not remembering names isn't a cause for alarm. While frustrating, it's normal and not a sign of major mental impairment.

Studies conducted at the University of Vermont have found that up to 60 percent of women report memory problems as they go through menopause, probably due to lower levels of a form of estrogen called *estradiol.* Additional research looking at nearly two thousand women at midlife over a six-year period published in *The American Journal of Epidemiology* found dips in memory, learning, and information processing speed were common.

Mara Mather, PhD, a cognitive psychologist at the University of California in Los Angeles, has shown in her research on emotion and memory that as we age, we tend to focus more on positive information and less on negative and prefer storing pleasant images rather than unpleasant ones. Her findings suggest that the increase in positivity is due to strategic processing that helps facilitate wellbeing. Mather has also shown that as we grow older, the amygdala, an almond-shaped group of cells buried deep within the brain responsible for emotions and motivation related to survival, also becomes less responsive to negative stimuli.

Yes, the brain shifts as we age. Neurons start to die before we are even born and continue to perish at an estimated rate of one cell a second every day for the rest of our lives. However, these changes don't mean you're deficient or staring down a double-barrel shotgun loaded with dementia. In fact, dementia rates are actually declining. While the absolute number is rising because people are living longer, total percentage rates are decreasing. According to a study published in *JAMA Internal Medicine* of over twenty-one thousand Americans sixty-five years or older, dementia rates fell by 24 percent from 11.6 percent in 2000 to 8.8 percent in 2012. Plus, there are many things you can do to decrease your dementia risk including maintaining a healthy weight and keeping your blood pressure, blood sugar, and cholesterol in the normal range. The whole foods plant-based diet discussed in Step 3 will help you with all four.

According to the MacArthur Foundation Research Network on Successful Aging, while losses may occur later in life, declines rarely impact all types of mental performance, and many older adults don't experience even minor losses of mental ability. In other words, your perceived mental deficiencies are probably not as bad as you believe. In addition, because certain aspects of your cognition are a little rusty, you think your entire mind is corroding.

While studies are light (college students and retirees are easier to recruit) and there is a tremendous amount of variation between individuals, research shows that at midlife we retain many of our abilities *and* even develop new ones. Thanks to the phenomenon of *neuroplasticity,* the one hundred billion brain cells you have rewire and reorganize themselves throughout your life incorporating new information, experiences, and behaviors.

Research from the Seattle Longitudinal Study, which followed the mental abilities of thousands of adults over the course of half a century, shows at midlife you use your brain in new ways and recruit additional parts to accomplish tasks. The brain's white matter, which is responsible for connecting nerve cells, peaks at forty or fifty. So while you may not remember where you parked your car (Don't worry. There's an app for that!), or how to solve quadratic equations (like you need that info, anyway) or diagram a sentence (start with a horizontal line and vertical line. Subject on the left, predicate on the right—easy!), you can earn that master's or learn French – *merci beaucoup!*

The Seattle Longitudinal Study found that at midlife, adults outperform younger counterparts on four out of six cognitive tests. While memorization skills and perceptual speed slow down, verbal and simple math abilities, along with spatial and abstract reasoning, improve.

Research on pilots and air traffic controllers has shown it can take longer for older adults to learn new things like using a flight simulator, but they do a better job at accomplishing important goals like avoiding crashes. I don't know about you, but I'll take being late over death any day!

IMPROVING YOUR MIND

There are measures you can take and strategies you can employ to boost brain health, improve memory and concentration, and bolster your thinking and positivity so you function efficiently and feel more confident socially. You may not roll like a Ferrari, but with a little mental tune-up, your brain can run like a trusty Toyota. The key is keeping three chemicals in balance—*serotonin* (responsible for feeling calm, optimistic, and confident), *dopamine* (responsible for keeping you motivated and energized), and *cortisol* (responsible for revving you up when necessary). Optimal balance can be achieved by managing your body and mind.

Here are ten specific techniques to reprogram your brain and improve your midlife memory and mood.

1. Relax. If you want to enhance your mind, the first step is to calm down. The anxiety, trepidation, and doom and gloom scenarios you may be painting can trigger a cortisol shit storm that truly will impair your mental abilities. Many researchers believe that elevated levels of cortisol, the hormone responsible for fight-or-flight, play a big role in altering the structure and chemical activities of the brain.

An animal study conducted at the University of Iowa and published in the *Journal of Neuroscience* found that surging levels of cortisol triggered by stress can lead to memory lapses as we age. As Jason Radley, a researcher on the paper explains, "Stress hormones are one mechanism that we believe leads to weathering of the brain. Like a rock on the shoreline, after years and years, it will eventually break down and disappear."

The quickest way to relax your body and mind and reduce stress is deep breathing. A couple of deep, cleansing breaths will power up your parasympathetic nervous system (aka the rest-and-digest system) and oxygenate your brain, making you feel more alert and awake. It's an easy, effective technique that requires no special equipment and only takes a minute or two. Simply take a deep breath through your nose, hold it for a moment, slowly exhale through your mouth, and repeat.

You can do it anywhere—at your desk, while you wait in line at the grocery store, or in your car. Just ten to fifteen minutes per day of deep breathing can improve how well your brain functions and reduce feelings of pain.

The biggest challenge is remembering to practice this powerful technique. Until it becomes a habit, set a reminder on your phone or computer to pause every hour and take a few moments to breathe. Deep breathing is a simple, effective way to clear your mind, boost your immune system, reduce stress, increase concentration, and improve your mood in moments.

There are an infinite number of other ways to relax your mind and body. Take a warm bath, listen to beautiful music, meditate, (Meditation has been shown to increase IQ, lower stress, and promote a higher level of brain functioning.) practice yoga, read, have a cup of tea, get a massage, take a walk in nature, journal, or use guided imagery.

ROCK YOUR MIDLIFE LAB
Just breathe

Breathing exercises are easy to learn and do, and can help generate calm while increasing your energy levels. When you don't have the space or time to nap, a minute or two of deep breathing is a great way to hit reset. You'll bathe your tissues, cells, and organs in oxygen and feel much fresher, less stressed, and more relaxed.

Two breathing exercises that you can try are belly breathing and box breathing.

Here's how to do belly breathing. Sit or lie in a comfortable position. Place one hand on your belly and one on your heart. Inhale deeply through your nose, allowing your belly to inflate and push against your hand. Exhale through pursed lips and experience your belly deflating. Repeat for three to ten rounds. This is great to do at bedtime to help you fall asleep.

"Box breathing" is so powerful that Navy SEALs use it to help them stay calm and focused. Here's how to do it: Inhale for four, hold your breath for four, exhale for four, and hold out for four. Repeat the sequence several times. If you are feeling stressed, extend the exhalation for a count of six. This will power up your rest-and-digest parasympathetic nervous system and calm down your fight-or-flight sympathetic nervous system.

2. Unplug. If you want to improve focus and concentration, reduce social media and overall electronics use. Messenger pings and Instagram dings create an addictive, distracting, compulsive pull that makes focusing difficult. Like a pathological gambler salivating at the racetrack, you release a hit of mesolimbic dopamine, the chief neuro-mediator of incentive motivation, each time your cellphone sounds. Dopamine highjacks your consciousness, shifting your focus to Facebook rather than the dinner you want to enjoy or the report that's due at 3 p.m.

Unplug at least an hour before you go to bed (the light emanating from your device interferes with your circadian rhythms and sleep), and don't leave your cellphone in your bedroom. If you really want to reboot your brain, go one full day a week phone-free.

Don't substitute TV for internet use, especially disturbing news programs. Your mom was right—it really is an idiot box, and our "if it bleeds it leads" news culture is designed to stress you out. While it can be disturbing to watch television, it is also so passive that it only burns twenty-three to thirty-three calories per hour. In contrast, reading burns thirty-four to fifty calories an hour; provides mental simulation, stress reduction, and vocabulary expansion; improves focus, thinking skills, and concentration, and may even fight Alzheimer's.

3. Enjoy brain-boosting activities. A big benefit of reducing electronic media use is gaining time to learn something new and do more activities you enjoy that nourish your brain and soul. Read a good novel. Play or listen to music. Studies have shown music strengthens the right hemisphere of the brain and alters its structure. Paint, draw, or knit. Develop a new hobby or skill like gardening, photography, dancing, or speaking a foreign language. Research shows sustained engagement over time in novel, demanding activities enhances memory.

4. Exercise. One of the best things you can do to get your gray matter in shape is to put down the digital brain-training games, like Lumosity and BrainHQ, and pick up some dumbbells. While purported to improve cerebral capacity, evidence showing they improve brain health is sparse and contradictory.

Being physically active changes the brain, enhancing memory and cognition. Exercise increases brain volume in the areas of the brain associated with reasoning and executive functioning and diminishes the impact of age-related brain changes on cognition. Studies show it is an effective way to reduce your risk of memory loss and Alzheimer's, even if you have a genetic risk for the disease.

Why is exercise so powerful? First, it increases your aerobic capacity, which in turn improves brain structure, function, and cognition. When you exercise, your heart rate increases, and more blood and oxygen flow to the brain—the most oxygen-hungry organ in the body. Being active also boosts levels of a protein called brain-derived neurotrophic factor (BDNF) that supports existing neurons and stimulates the growth of new ones. It also improves brain health directly by reducing inflammation and insulin resistance. Plus, it improves sleep, which has a positive impact on your brain.

Not only does exercise reduce stress and anxiety but it also acts as an antidepressant and promotes the release of endorphins, which produce the famous "runner's high." It also releases other mood boosting neurotransmitters like serotonin. Studies have also shown that exercise is as powerful as Prozac. A review published in the ACSM's (American College of Sports Medicine) *Health and Fitness Journal* concluded that exercise appears to be an effective treatment for depression, improving depressive symptoms to a comparable extent as pharmacotherapy and psychotherapy. While more research is needed to determine how much exercise is required to positively impact mood, studies suggest that ninety minutes per week (thirty minutes, three times per week) is enough to reduce symptoms.

5. Eat right. Your brain is a glutton, consuming more energy than any other organ. Although it's only the size of two fists and weighs about three pounds, it uses approximately 420 calories a day in the form of glucose, roughly 60 percent of the body's stores. Since it can't store energy to work properly, your brain requires a steady supply of blood sugar to power the transmission of nerve impulses and a complex cascade of chemicals derived from the nutrients you eat. If you're living on diet cola and "energy bars" or skipping meals completely, your brain isn't going to function properly.

One of the best diets for the brain and overall health is the Mediterranean diet. It's similar to the whole foods plant-based diet discussed in the last chapter, but recommends eating seafood twice a week. Studies have found that a diet rich in fish, whole grains, green leafy vegetables, olive oil, and nuts can reduce the risk of Alzheimer's and help to maintain brain health.

The Mediterranean diet is rich in the omega-3 fatty acids, DHA and EPA, which have been shown to improve focus, memory, and learning, and reduce the risk of depression and mood disorders. Omega 3s are found in fatty fish like salmon and tuna, and in walnuts and flaxseeds, and can also be taken as a supplement.

While more studies are needed to prove their brain benefits, taking vitamins C (500 mg), D (get tested to determine your blood level), and E (400 IUs) have been shown to improve brain health.

Eating foods chockfull of antioxidants can also help reduce inflammation and slow brain aging. Good choices include leafy greens and cruciferous vegetables (kale, spinach, cabbage, and broccoli); berries; certain spices (turmeric, cinnamon, and ginger); and dark chocolate. Three beverages—coffee, tea, and red wine— may also benefit brain health. Coffee has been shown to improve memory and may diminish dementia risk. Caffeine in coffee and tea can also stimulate the brain, improving focus and cognition. Tea and red wine are rich in antioxidants that may reduce cell damage associated with aging. In addition, red wine contains a phytochemical called *resveratrol,* which may decrease the promotion of plaques that can harm the brain.

To optimize how your brain works and reduce the risk of disease, eat a healthy breakfast to provide a steady supply of energy to your brain. Limiting your intake of sugar, (Studies show diets high in sugar are linked to poorer memory and lower total brain volume.), alcohol (it's a neurotoxin), and foods high in saturated fats like red meat and full-fat dairy products can also support brain health. Try to maintain a healthy weight. A number of studies have found an association between obesity and the risk of cognitive decline.

Your brain and how you feel are also affected by the production of *serotonin*, a neurotransmitter that inhibits pain and aids the regulation of sleep and moods. While it affects the brain, serotonin production occurs mostly in your intestinal tract, so improving gut health can help to increase your levels and improve mood.

There are several simple things you can do to support your gut (see the previous Step 3 for tips to boost gut microbiome health and balance). Try eating a diet that's high in plant foods and low in processed foods, sugar, and saturated fats for two weeks and notice how you feel. You may also want to try adding fermented foods like yogurt, kombucha, pickles, and sauerkraut to your diet or taking a probiotic supplement. Studies demonstrate that taking a probiotic supplement may reduce anxiety and perception of stress, and improve mental outlook.

One more dietary technique that may help is chewing gum. One piece of Trident or Wrigley's may boost activity in the *hippocampus,* a part of the brain involved in storing memories. While research is contradictory, one study presented at a meeting of the British Psychological Society showed that people who chewed gum had a higher level of accuracy and reaction times while completing a memory recall task. Chewing gum may also help improve focus and attention by increasing oxygen flow to the brain.

6. Sleep well. Getting a good night's rest is one of the most important things you can do to improve memory and support mental health. That's because memories are consolidated when you sleep, essentially moved from temporary storage in the hippocampus to more permanent storage in the neocortex. So if you're short on Zs, your recall will suffer.

One study showed that participants who napped and then were asked to memorize a set of cards recalled 85 percent of the patterns compared to controls who only remembered 60 percent.

7. Be mindful. Cellphones and software that allow us to externalize our memory by recording infinite bits of info are changing us. We've become cognitive couch potatoes and gotten soft in the memory department. Fortunately, just like you can strengthen a muscle by lifting weights, you can strengthen neural connections by making a conscious effort to consolidate memories—transferring them from short-term to long-term storage—so they can be recalled in the future.

Research shows that *mindfulness,* a practice popularized by Jon Kabat-Zinn that entails developing moment-to-moment awareness without judgment, can improve memory and reduce mind-wandering. A study published in *Brain Imaging and Behavior* showed that mindfulness training is associated with both enhanced growth of the hippocampus (the part of the brain involved in remembering information) and an increase in working memory.

You've learned a bit about mindfulness in Step 2 when it came up in the discussion of self-compassion and the work of Kristin Neff. You'll learn much more about mindfulness and how to practice it in Step 7. For now, start by slowing down and focusing on one thing at a time. Select a daily, routine activity or two (such as brushing your teeth, taking a shower, walking to your car, or eating breakfast) to intentionally practice on. Do nothing else but the activity and use all five senses to focus on what you see, hear, taste, touch, and smell as you perform it. A few minutes a day is powerful.

After my incident with my friend Jill on the dance floor, I made a decision to focus on improving my memory, especially my ability to remember names by being more mindful. When I meet someone new, I try to associate their name with an object that rhymes with their name. Then I visualize them interacting with the item. For example, I see my new friend Charlie riding a Harley or my new associate Jane sitting in a plane.

When I spend time with people, I turn my phone off and turn on my presence. I pay attention, listen intently, and treat that person with respect. Through my words and actions, I connect and demonstrate how much I value and am interested in them.

Following the advice of motivational speaker Nancy Mathew, Founder of Visions in Action, Inc. and author of *The One Philosophy,* I treat everyone as if they are The One—the next most important person I want to meet.

Here are a few other ways to use mindfulness to improve memory. Pause throughout your day for a few minutes and notice whatever you are doing, whether that's sitting in front of a computer, eating lunch, or scanning your phone. When you encounter new info, take a moment to deliberately differentiate the latest information from older material. Be easy with yourself and take your time when you are trying to learn something new.

For more on mindfulness training, check out any books by Jon Kabat-Zinn or a Mindfulness-Based Stress Reduction (MBSR) or a Mindful Self-compassion (MSC) course. (Resources are listed in the back of this book.)

8. Declutter Mentally. At midlife, there's so much to do and focus on that you can easily feel stressed and overwhelmed, which can turn your brain into a muddled mess. Fortunately, there's a solution. Just like you clean out your closets, garage, and dusty drawers, you can declutter your mind.

ROCK YOUR MIDLIFE LAB
Fear dump

Pull out your *Rock Your Midlife Playbook*[i] or journal and write down anything and everything that's bothering you. Get it all out—the worries, fears, doubts, pent-up emotions, and everything you feel you have to do. Trust me, this really works. Research published in the *Journal of Experimental Psychology* found "expressive writing reduces intrusive and avoidant thoughts about negative events and improves working memory."

Then to release your emotions, talk to a good friend, loved one, coach, or therapist who can offer a new perspective and help you come up with solutions to your problems.

Once your mind is clearer, prioritize. Figure out what's most important to you. Turn to a fresh page in your journal or *Rock Your Midlife Playbook*[i], and write out your long-term goals. Next list action steps that can help you get there. Order the steps and start attacking them.

The key is to *stop* procrastinating and start taking action. Make some decisions.

Putting things off and being indecisive gums up your mind with overwhelm. Can't decide what to do? Flip a coin or visualize path A and path B, and determine which choice feels better.

Still feeling stuck? Declutter your desk. A study published in the *Journal of Consumer Research* found that when faced with a challenging situation people who have a messy work space are more frustrated, inefficient, tired, and less persistent.

9. Ditch multitasking. I know what you're thinking: Doing a million things simultaneously increases productivity. That's a complete myth. Research from Stanford University found that heavy multitasking reduces efficiency and can impair cognitive control.

Writing your work presentation while watching the news and making supper is like plugging the toaster, microwave, and washer-dryer into the same outlet. Not only will you blow a brain fuse, but you'll also increase stress and decrease attention span.

Slowing down and doing *only* one thing at a time is an easy, straightforward step, but it's incredibly hard to turn into a habit because we're so used to juggling.

To free up brain space, write down everything you need to do. Then order your list and discipline yourself to do one thing at a time.

10. Think positive. It's estimated that we have approximately sixty thousand thoughts a day—that's forty-one thoughts a minute! And they aren't always fresh and positive. As I discussed in Chapter 2, we ruminate, often replaying the same old negative tapes: *I'm not good enough. My life would be better if I had more money, a bigger house, a better spouse, or a new job. I'm too old to...*

To review: It's not your fault. It's neuroscience. As previously mentioned, we humans have a *negativity bias* to protect us from potential danger. This means your mind tends to focus on worry, fear, and doubt, rather than positive emotions like love, compassion, inspiration, pride, hope, or gratitude that build resilience and broaden awareness so you can grow. Since you become what you think about all day, you don't move forward personally or professionally. Negative thoughts generate difficult emotions, which trigger negative behaviors. Rather than making your next chapter your best chapter, you stay stuck and find experiencing joy, purpose, and meaning elusive.

Psychologist Rick Hanson in *Hardwiring Happiness* suggests upending the negativity bias by "Savoring the Good." Savoring entails being mindful when positive or pleasant experiences occur. Rather than plowing forward, slow down when something good happens or you're enjoying yourself and savor it. When your kid shares good news, you're out on a beautiful nature walk, or spending time with someone you love, take it all in using all your senses.

Like gratitude (appreciating the good things in your life), research conducted at the University of Pennsylvania shows that savoring joys and pleasures greatly increases happiness and life satisfaction. Additional research published in the scientific journal *Neuron* found that recalling and savoring happy memories evokes pleasant feelings and positive emotions associated with the original experience. The research suggests, "recalling positive autobiographical memories is intrinsically valuable, which may be adaptive for regulating positive emotion and promoting better wellbeing."

According to psychologist Barbara Frederickson, author of *Positivity: Discover the Upward Spiral That Will Change Your Life*, to have a good life we need a 3:1 ratio of positive to negative emotions.

You can elevate the number of positive emotions you experience each day with this simple Attention Exercise. When you notice your thoughts are going south, pay attention to what you are paying attention to (yes, practice mindfulness!). Ask yourself: *What do I notice in my immediate environment, what thought am I thinking, and is it positive, negative, or neutral.* Positive thoughts are expansive, neutral thoughts feel neither expansive nor contractive, and negative thoughts feel contractive. Then see if you can change how you are feeling by changing the focus of your attention. Focus more on neutral or positive thoughts and interrupt negative thoughts and feelings by shifting your attention.

ROCK YOUR MIDLIFE LAB:
The ABC Model of Optimism

A proven way to be more positive is to practice the ABC Model of Learned Optimism. Developed by psychologist Martin Seligman, the father of positive psychology, the model will help you unearth and change the underlying thoughts that influence your behaviors by challenging them.

In the model, *A* stands for Adversity, *B* for Belief, *C* for Consequences, *D* for Disputation, and *E* for Energization. Here's how it works:

A: Recall a recent Adverse event. For example, imagine you have been trying to eat healthier and slipped up and ate several donuts.

B: Note the Beliefs that come up. For example: I

have no willpower; I'll never lose weight; I'm no good at eating right.

C: Consider the Consequences of your beliefs. Do you feel like a failure, and want to quit working on yourself and eat another donut or two?

D: Dispute the beliefs that came up from the adverse event by looking for examples that disprove your beliefs and change your assumptions. For example, think about all the other times you made healthier choices or other places in your life where you set a goal, took action, and reached it.

E: Notice how you feel now that you've disputed your beliefs. Do you feel more motivated, hopeful, and energized?

Anyone can learn to be more optimistic, and there are numerous benefits, including having a healthier body and mind, longevity, reduced stress, and increased motivation. Try the model for yourself. While this is an ongoing process, with practice you'll start to see the world from a happier place and be able to attract positive opportunities resulting in more fortunate outcomes.

Congratulations, you've made it through Step 4. How do you feel? What did you learn? What concrete steps will you use going forward to gain more clarity and calm?

Continue to work on your mind and stay positive. Focusing your thoughts is key to rocking your midlife because what you think about you bring about. Your thoughts create your feelings. Your feelings create your actions, and those actions determine how your next chapter will unfold.

Which brings us to our next chapter: Step 5: Empower Yourself, where you will learn to conquer the biggest roadblock: *fear*. Turn the page and let's get you to start attracting what you want in your life.

CHAPTER SUMMARY:

- Being more forgetful at midlife is normal and can be a blessing.
- We trade some of our cognitive capacity for love and wisdom and become more tranquil and positive as we age.
- There are numerous techniques and strategies you can employ to improve how your mind functions, including relaxing, unplugging from media, exercising, and eating a healthy diet.

7

STEP #5: EMPOWER YOURSELF: FROM HELPLESS TO IN CHARGE

Men are much simpler mechanisms than women.
Nothing changes them ...even when they have a
midlife crisis, they do it in a mindless way... that's
why I think we should let men go off and have affairs
and drive fast cars and dream of being virile –
and we should run the world.

— Goldie Hawn

When I first started working with my client, Linda, she was stuck and going through a hellish metamorphosis.

"I just want to create the space within for my next steps after a devastating divorce," she told me during our first call. "I feel stuck and don't know what to do next. I want to move forward, date again, get my health on track, and eliminate procrastination, but I don't know how to go about it."

What a horrible divorce it was. After twenty years of marriage, her husband came home from work one afternoon, told her out of the blue that he wanted a divorce, and proceeded to pack a duffle bag. A classic runaway husband (a term coined by family therapist Vikki Stark), he was having an affair with his massage therapist and wanted out of his marriage so he could move in with her. Suddenly, rather than loving and caring, he was distant and aggressive. Completely blindsided, Linda was the devastated, bewildered, abandoned wife in need of recovery and renewal.

And then… the universe threw Linda another nasty curve ball. Her BRCA gene test, a blood test done to analyze DNA and identify harmful changes (mutations) in cancer susceptibility genes, was positive. Like actress Angelina Jolie, who underwent a preventive double mastectomy and oophorectomy (removal of the ovaries), Linda had a high risk of getting breast and/or ovarian cancer.

After constant contemplation and nightmarish rumination, Linda made the decision to have her breasts and ovaries removed. It was an empowering choice that saved her life. An analysis of the organs that were removed revealed the presence of precancerous cells that, if left untreated, would have turned into full-blown cancer.

The decision to take charge of her health, rather than tempt fate, transformed Linda from a devastated housewife into an empowered woman. Rather than be a victim, she took charge of her body, mind, heart, spirit, and relationships.

Empowerment had a snowball effect. Linda went from stuck and unhappy to free and energized. Along the way she learned to trust the universe and build confidence as she took step after step forward squarely on her next chapter path. Sure she still had struggles—who doesn't at midlife—but she developed a new life and identity and an independence (this was her first time being on her own in decades) that was delicious.

She was seeking individual agency, and that's exactly what she received.

Here's where her empowerment journey took her: trading the stability and stasis of being a wife and stay-at-home mom who raised three kids, for a demanding, volatile day job and a side hustle beauty business. To reduce her cancer risk and get back in shape, she transformed her diet, swapping her daily wine and cheese habit for juicing and a high-fiber, plant-based diet. Watching Netflix was exchanged for studying Spanish and earning certifications to expand professionally. Credit card bills got paid off, and she consulted a financial advisor to nail her financial freedom. She began feeling difficult emotions and showing forgiveness and grace to her ex-husband, even though he didn't deserve it.

In our last session together, she told me: "I feel empowered that I took control over my health and my finances. I've learned to go with my gut and listen to my intuition. I'm standing up for myself. I'm living in thriving mode and not in victim or survival mode. I have control over my destiny—not just deciding what I want for my life, but acting on it. I am finally coming out of who I was and beginning to live who I want to be."

Oh yes, and I almost forgot, after her struggles and realizing how few resources are out there for women with difficult genetic screenings, Linda is writing a book about being a *previvor:* someone who has a high risk of developing cancer but has not been diagnosed and typically has challenging health decisions to make. She's excited to share her story and knowledge and inspire and empower other women. I can't wait to read it.

WHAT IS EMPOWERMENT?

Empowerment is a noun, a thing, like a slice of chocolate cake or a kitten. The Oxford Dictionary defines empowerment as "authority or power given to someone to do something" and "the process of becoming stronger and more confident, especially in controlling one's life and claiming one's rights."

I love the second part of the definition because it makes clear that empowerment isn't a one-shot-and-you're-done deal. Like all the steps you are taking to rock your midlife, empowerment is a process. You don't work your empowerment muscle only once to get stronger. Whether you're building biceps or glutes, you have to stress the muscles involved in curling your arm or moving your hip by lifting heavier and heavier weights. This stress creates tiny tears in the muscle fibers. With rest and proper nutrition, your muscles grow back bigger and stronger, and you show up energized, toned, and confident.

In the same way, to grow stronger internally you have to stress and nourish your empowerment muscles. The end result is that you trust yourself more and feel in control of your work and world. You trade being a victim for being the heroine and author of your story.

How do you do that? It's an inside-out process that starts with believing in yourself and developing an empowered mindset and vibe. The word *empowerment* means "power from within." In contrast, the word *power* connotes "power over" something, that force being external, from without.

Like a tiger, rather than a sheep, you get fierce. When life hits you with a rotting curve ball, you come out swinging, and you don't let adversity break you. You face your fears, consult your inner wisdom, and make hard choices. To quote an aphorism attributed to the 19th-century German philosopher Friedrich Nietzsche (or pop star Kelly Clarkson), "What doesn't kill you makes you stronger."

ROCK YOUR MIDLIFE LAB

What does empowerment mean to you?

Part of becoming empowered means drilling down and determining what empowerment means to you, so grab your journal or *Rock Your Midlife Playbook*[i] and start writing your definition. Then take an inventory and write down all the things that make you feel empowered.

Here are a few things my followers and clients have told me:

- "The ability to make my own choices empowers me. It can still be crazy but even just knowing that I can make a choice if I want to gives me a lift."

- "Giving from my own overflow with boundaries, standards, and limits—safe, sane, and consensually."

- "I'm empowered by trying new things and having new experiences—whether or not they're successful. It's less about the goal than having new experiences."

- "I find it empowering when I live by my own rules and values, and stand up for myself! Disempowering when I listen to opinions of others about how my life should be and cave-in."

- "Community, self-reflection, embodied movement, mindful living, and making conscious choices are all deeply empowering for me! Yay Chakra 3!"

- Other words women have shared with me about empowerment include my faith, exercise, patience, helping others, my friends, and family members.

AUTHENTICITY + LOA = EMPOWERMENT ENERGY

Being authentic (what you learned in Step 1) plus harnessing the Law of Attraction is the formula for how you strengthen your empowerment muscle. The combo is your membership to the empowerment gym where you build the muscle and mojo needed to steer your path towards becoming the star of your life.

The Law of Attraction (LOA), as you may recall, is the belief that you attract into your life whatever you give your energy and attention to. You harness it by doing three things: ask, believe, and receive. You ask for what you want, believe you can have it, and remain open to receiving what you requested. If you focus your energy on empowering thoughts, beliefs, and actions, you'll attract more positive people and things into your life. Conversely, if you feel disempowered and dwell on thoughts and situations that drain you and make you feel angry, stressed, or sad, you'll attract more of the same.

That's why I can't emphasize enough the importance of *feeling* like a star. Referencing the Star card in Tarot, when you become the star of your life, you feel inspired and are filled with hope, faith, and a sense of purpose. Life feels magical, and anything and everything is possible. Even after turmoil (The Star card follows The Tower, which represents destruction and abrupt change), you feel blessed and serene in the way Noah must have felt when a dove carrying an olive branch and followed by a rainbow appeared.

Able to harness both your intuition and intellect, you open your heart, show up as your true self, and shine. Yes, you may feel vulnerable exposing who you are to the world (the woman pictured in the Star card is naked).

Taking off the protective masks that block your starlight takes courage. In a world that worships youth and flawlessness, accepting your imperfect self exactly as you are is an empowering, brave, audacious act.

Self-acceptance is imperative for your empowered, next chapter metamorphosis. To paraphrase psychologist Carl Rogers,

"Staying vulnerable is a risk we have to take if we want to experience connection."

—Brené Brown

the curious paradox is that when you accept yourself just as you are, then you can change. You must start where you are.

This doesn't mean that you don't make an effort to transform yourself and your life or allow yourself to be treated badly. Instead, you observe what is going on inside and out. You notice how you are feeling about yourself and your life. Rather than judging or rejecting your experience or putting up walls to keep difficult, confusing emotions out, you accept what is happening *now*. You give yourself permission to feel everything—sadness, pain, frustration, anger, joy, and pleasure—and practice self-compassion when difficult emotions arise. You let go of needing things to be a certain way and accept what is. Basically, you stop fighting life and start swimming with the tide. In doing so, you simultaneously accept the things you don't like about midlife and embrace the increase in wisdom, wellbeing, and positive emotions that you experience.

Self-acceptance will help you feel good in your skin and show up empowered in your life. You'll harness the Law of Attraction because you'll see opportunities for growth and expansion in the present moment, which is the only time there is. The old limiting beliefs that kept you stuck in your disempowered state will disappear, creating space for new, empowered ones to appear.

Encouraging the Law of Attraction to help you manifest what you want is like gardening. Thoughts lay down the blueprint of what you want, and emotions are the magnetic energy that attracts it to you. You have to pull out the old negative weeds in your mind, plant positive thoughts in fertile soil, and water them daily with positive emotions so they don't dry up. The more you allow positive emotions, rather than fear and negativity, to dominate your life, the more empowered you will become.

According to the Law of Attraction, as you strengthen and stretch your empowerment muscle, you will start to know and ask for what you truly want (which you uncovered in Step 1), and those things will show up. As you receive what you want with gratitude and open arms, keep up the positive self-talk, and learn to savor the good in your life, more blessings will appear.

However, you must be patient. As you transform your vibration, it takes time for the outside world to catch up to the longings in your heart that feel so real. Keep visualizing the new wonderful job, loving relationship, healthier body, beautiful home… Believe it's there in your future and be open to receive it—or something even better.

What's interesting and exciting about the LOA manifestation process is that you eventually get to the point where the present is always perfect. You don't want more because everything you want is right here, right now.

Yes, there are still big problems in the world, and you will still have personal problems, *but* when you are grateful, present, and mindful, you love the mess too.

It goes back to the *wabi-sabi* life we talked about in Step 2. You see and even learn to love the flaws and imperfections. For example, the things in your partner that once drove you crazy can be perceived as charming, and presto, you have a wonderful spouse. Or that credit card debt—it's an opportunity to improve your relationship with money and focus on abundance and attaining financial freedom, not lack. War, hunger, and environmental problems are a little trickier, but it all comes down to Gandhi's encouragement to "be the change you want to see in the world." You can donate money to a cause, volunteer, write a letter to your senator, but in the process, you will inspire and empower others. (More on all of this in Step 7: Enlighten Yourself.)

ROCK YOUR MIDLIFE LAB
Overcoming Imposter Syndrome

Do you sometimes feel like a fraud or fake? No matter how much you do or progress, no matter how many people say you're amazing or how hard you try, you fear being unmasked as a phony.

You're not alone. Many of us, especially women who grew up in families that emphasized achievement, suffer from Imposter Syndrome, a pervasive feeling of insecurity and self-doubt. What's ironic is that Imposter Syndrome doesn't strike losers. Rather it impacts smart, successful people—often after they've just reached their Everest. Sheryl Sandberg, Tina Fey, and Serena Williams all admit that they've felt like frauds.

While it's not classified as a mental disorder, Imposter Syndrome is often accompanied by anxiety, stress, or depression. It's typically associated with perfectionism and thoughts like: *I feel like a fake, I must not fail,* or *I'm just lucky.*

What's tragic is that when you internalize the message *I am a fake,* that's how you show up in the world. And the consequences are huge. To protect yourself from being unmasked, you self-sabotage and rob yourself and the world of your unique gifts and greatness. Instead of shining, you suffer mentally and emotionally and don't experience the success, abundance, and wealth that you crave. You repel what you want, discombobulating the Law of Attraction.

Along with shining your light, there are several things you can do to overcome Imposter Syndrome.

- Practice mindfulness. It deactivates the Default Mode Network (DMN), a network of brain areas that becomes active when the mind is resting and disengaged. The DMN looks for what's wrong in your environment (which includes being unmasked as a fake), creates a sense of self, and sees that self in the past or future.
- Focus on and lift up others.
- When someone compliments you say, "Thank you."
- Practice self-compassion. Unlike self-esteem, which fluctuates widely because it's an evaluation of your worth, self-compassion is steady and reliable.
- Look yourself in the mirror every day and say, "I am enough."
- Be you! No one can tell you you're doing it wrong.

THE EMPOWERMENT— SELF-COMPASSION CONNECTION

As Kristin Neff explains in her book, *Fierce Self-compassion: How Women Can Harness Kindness to Speak Up, Claim Their Power and Thrive*, "Self-compassion is aimed at alleviating suffering, and to do so, sometimes we need to protect ourselves—to speak up, say no, draw boundaries, or to stand up to injustice."

By engaging the yang side of your self-compassion muscle and the empowerment mindset, you can see difficulties as challenges that teach you things to help you grow and glow. This resilience in turn feeds empowerment. You view setbacks, failures, and misfortune as stepping stones that lead to success. You bring in the common humanity element of self-compassion and view hardships and challenges as a normal part of life. All of which foster *resilience*—the ability to recover quickly from misfortune or challenges.

You affirm: *Everything is happening for my highest good.* As Linda demonstrated, you become preemptive rather than reactive. Like a martial artist, you train in defensive tactics and protect yourself from harm. After break-ups, health issues, or career stumbling blocks, you put the pieces of your life back together with self-compassion duct tape. You call for backup from people and rituals that help you heal and connect with the highest most empowered energy there is—love. Empowerment is kryptonite for being stuck. It's the fire in your belly that keeps you motivated, challenged, and moving forward.

ROCK YOUR MIDLIFE LAB:
Strike a power pose

Not feeling like an empowered star yet? According to Amy Cuddy, a Harvard professor and author of *Presence: Bringing Your Boldest Self to Your Biggest Challenges,* you can access your personal power by changing your body language. Cuddy's research suggests that our body language impacts how we think and feel about ourselves. In other words, how you hold your body can impact your mind. To feel empowered, she recommends adopting a high power pose for a few minutes: instead of hunching over and making yourself small, stretch out star-like with legs spread and arms in a V and make yourself big.

Since emotions are felt in the body, you can connect with your star power and attract good energy anytime anywhere by assuming Goddess (in yoga) or Horse (in martial arts) stance. Simply stand up, spread your legs wider than hip-distance with feet turned out. Squat down and bend your elbows at a 90-degree angle. Not only will you turn on and tone your thighs, core, and lower body, you'll feel physically and psychologically empowered. That self-concept and inner energy alone will ground and center you, so you can support and protect yourself and move forward powerfully with *author*-ity.

Since you are the *author*-ity of your own story, it can be helpful to write out the narrative of your life in which you are the star as the empowered heroine. Here's my tale, followed by a guided journaling opportunity for you to write your own empowerment story.

MY EMPOWERMENT STORY

Like Persephone, queen of the underworld, wife of Hades, and goddess of spring growth, I've been through hell and back a couple of times. Like most women, I bet you have too.

Four months after leaving my ex-husband, my retina detached three times, plunging me into blackness. If left untreated, the detachments would lead to blindness. The disease struck my good eye, the right peeper with the 20/20 vision. Ironically, I had just undergone cataract surgery in that eye and was seeing beautifully for the first time in years.

Prior to surgery, my optometrist suggested I postpone the operation as long as possible. "You never know what might happen," she warned.

Ah, the joys of midlife. No matter how well you care for your body, *shit happens.*

I was showering after a sweaty, Sunday morning workout. I bent at the waist to towel dry my hair. When I stood up pinprick-sized, black dots and large squiggles resembling bugs appeared. I blinked, closed my eyes, administered eye drops, told myself the spots were a figment of my imagination and willed the specks to disappear. But nothing erased the spots.

Maybe it was stress. After all, I was going through a contentious divorce. That afternoon, I was meeting my ex at my son's band concert to get my mail, and the thought of seeing him triggered anxiety. Perhaps a relaxing evening after the show and a good night's sleep would restore my eye.

Wondering what was going on, I consulted Google. I typed "floaters" in the search bar. The National Eye Institute described my problem: *Floaters are little "cobwebs" or specks that float about in your field of vision. They are small, dark, shadowy shapes that can look like spots, thread-like strands, or squiggly lines. They move as your eyes move and seem to dart away when you try to look at them directly.*

Eye issues have plagued me my entire life. At three, I was diagnosed with myopia that progressed into extreme nearsight-edness. My mom, whose eye issues I inherited, bought me my first pair of glasses—ridiculous, light blue, cat-eye frames encrusted with rhinestones. I loved them, and so did Mom because, while over-the-top, she knew if I liked them, I'd wear them.

On Monday, I called my retinal specialist, Dr. Schwartz, who I had been seeing for years for thinning retinas. He examined my eye and said, "What you're experiencing is a normal part of the aging process. The vitreous, a gel-like substance in your eye, has shrunk becoming stringy and casting shadows on your retina. It won't go away, but your brain will get used to them so you won't perceive them anymore."

He instructed me to go easy on the exercise—no jumping, jogging, or heavy lifting—call if I noticed vision changes, and come back in a month.

A week later my eyesight started to fail. A black curtain was closing across my field of vision making it impossible to see anything but a little light and objects right in front of my face. I called Schwartz who told me to come in immediately.

The news was bad: "You have a detached retina. If we don't do something immediately you'll go blind," he said.

The news and need to operate *now* triggered a panic attack and a massive hot flash. I had absolutely no control over what was happening. I removed my sweater, sipped water, ate almonds to raise my blood sugar, and tried to compose myself.

Dr. Schwartz prepared for a freeze treatment called *cryopexy* to weld my eye back in place. "Ready?" he asked, shooting my face-up with a numbing agent. He then inserted a gas bubble to push my retina back in place and finally injected the freezing agent, which would make a scar around the tear in my retina and once healed help keep it in place again.

"This will feel a bit like an ice cream headache," he told me, stabbing my eye.

An assistant taped up my eye, and Dr. Schwartz sent me home with instructions for "positioning." Positioning is a lovely term for lying in a specific, single position for nineteen to twenty hours per day to allow the gas bubble to cover the welding site, so the retina can heal.

The next day I returned to the doctor's office and received good news. My retina had reattached. I celebrated with more

"It is important to expect nothing, to take every experience, including the negative ones, as merely steps on the path, and to proceed."

—Ram Dass

"positioning," digesting four episodes of *The Crown,* five of *Orange Is the New Black,* and two documentaries on Ram Dass.

On Friday, my retina was still attached, but over the weekend my sight started failing. I panicked as my field of vision and psyche blackened. What would happen if I lost sight? How would I work, drive, live....

I returned to the doctor's office and learned that my retina was detached again. Remaining optimistic and wanting to avoid the operating room, Schwartz did another *cryopexy* and sent me home for more positioning. By Friday my retina was reattached, but over the weekend the shadows returned. This time the *macula,* an area near the center of the retina responsible for color vision, was impacted. Time to operate.

The word *operate* was the trigger for complete surrender. Lying on the gurney waiting for the anesthesiologist to injected me with a sleep cocktail, I had nothing left to do. This was my breakthrough moment. I relinquished control, let go of fear, and held on to trust. My eyes were in Dr. Schwartz and God's hands. As I drifted asleep, I silently affirmed, *Everything is happening for my highest good.*

Schwartz "threw the kitchen sink" at my eye, performing every procedure in his toolbox. Post-op, I woke up face down in the recovery room, my head supported by a purple, foam pillow. I remembered nothing after being wheeled into the O.R. and felt pretty good, considering I had just had general anesthesia. The nurse monitoring my vitals handed me chocolate pudding and encouraged me to drink water.

For the next week, I lay on a black massage table, "positioning" face down for twenty hours a day, watching Netflix and the Gaia channel on a ThinkPad. I'm an exercise junkie and love movement, so getting through each day was difficult, but I had no choice. Fortunately, the retina reattached.

Initially, my vision was blurry. I was able to detect light and some movement. No one was sure how well I'd eventually see. Months went by. I kept the faith and healed. I was lucky. My eyesight, while not perfect, is very good, probably better than the doctor had hoped for.

On the surface, dealing with my detached retina was a nightmare, but seeing silver linings empowered me. Suffering teaches you important life lessons, lessons you wouldn't have learned otherwise. Challenges and fear force you to go deep inside and discover resources and insights that you didn't know you had. By searching for the positive and working on patience and trust, you generate inner peace and can better respond to future situations rather than react. This empowers you and puts you in a better position to solve problems and support yourself. If there's no solution, you can accept what is, adapt, and grow.

My detached retina taught me about gratitude, prayer, healing, compassion, faith, and love. I've learned to stay balanced, focused, and positive, and move forward toward my dreams and goals even when faced with illness and loss. I've deepened my spiritual practice (more on that in Step 7) with a combination of Reiki (a type of energy healing) and Mindful Self-compassion. Practicing self-Reiki and following the Five Reiki Precepts (spiritual guidelines that promote wellbeing and help practitioners embody Reiki energy) was soothing and restorative. Years of meditating and offering myself compassion have taught me how to be kind rather than judgmental towards myself, and take things moment-by-moment and day-by-day.

Ultimately, my health crisis was empowering. Ironically, almost going blind taught me to see clearly. I learned how to turn off the fearful voices in my head, the shadow self that lives in a world of depression and anxiety and is constantly looking for what is wrong in life rather than what is right. I've learned that I am in charge of my happiness and can be joyful no matter what.

BE YOUR OWN AUTHOR-ITY

You are the heroine of your own story. Own that fact. It will empower you to believe in yourself, step up when challenges appear, dig deep, face your fears, never let others bring you down, and keep on truckin'.

As sociologist Joseph Campbell explains in his book *The Hero With a Thousand Faces,* you, my dear heroine are on a JOurneY. In Act I, you start out in your ordinary world and are called to adventure. Perhaps you refuse until… you meet a mentor (face-to-face, virtually, or through reading a book) who helps you step outside your comfort zone and begin your quest. In Act II, you enter a special world where you're tested. "Yuck, please do we really have to go there?" you may say. Sorry, sister. It's a necessary part of the process. No mud, no lotus.

You meet allies and enemies and come face-to-face with all your demons—the doubts and fears that keep you up at night. Breathe and reflect because you'll need even more courage to meet the supreme ordeal—a dangerous test or deep inner crisis that you have to overcome in order to save yourself or the world you came from.

The good news is that you make it through the darkness and discover the light. Transformed and rewarded, you are strong and empowered. You can now return home a changed woman and share your life-affirming knowledge with others so they too can transform.

This is the classic story arc of mythic heroines like Alice in Wonderland and Dorothy Gale of *The Wizard of Oz,* both of whom leave home, face confusion and enemies, and ultimately return home. It's the tale of movie characters like Buffy the Vampire Slayer; Ripley in *Aliens,* and Disney's brave, strong, compassionate Moana. It's stories of strong women who faced challenges and struggles, like Oprah Winfrey, Michelle Obama, Malala Yousafzai, and Helen Keller.

ROCK YOUR MIDLIFE LAB
What's your story?

You have a story too. Let's discover it together and use what you find to help you build up your empowerment muscle.

Me? I can't rub two words together, let alone write, you may be thinking.

Actually, you, like all humans are a story-telling animal. Humans have been gathering around fires (okay, these days more like screens and stages) for millennia sharing stories of triumph and tragedy.

Your words, experience, and narrative are powerful. Telling your story, especially if you see it retrospectively with the 20/20 vision of love and wisdom, can help you understand yourself and move forward with courage and strength.

It's your story, so you can't tell it wrong. Plus, you can upgrade it or give it an alternative ending. The point isn't to get it "right" but to use your story to uncover and discover higher truths about yourself and the world. Being an empowered storyteller, speaking the truth of your story, and aligning it with the purpose and passion you discovered in Step 1 will empower you to be the *author*-ity of your life.

Grab your journal or *Rock Your Midlife Playbook*[i], and let's get started.

1. Write out five to ten defining moments of your life. For example, the day you were born, your 13th birthday, first period, high school or college graduation, the death of a friend or pet, birth of your first child, a health crisis or scare, the day

you met your beloved, where you were when you heard about 9/11, your first big international trip, the day you got a big promotion after much struggle.

2. Pick one story that stands out that you'd like to examine now. It doesn't have to be the most difficult or dramatic. Recall the story in your mind's eye. Who was there, how did you feel, what happened? What did you learn? When you're ready, begin to write for at least ten minutes. Share how you grew. Look for the empowering moments when you were strong and courageous. Where did you heal and transform? You can even give an alternative ending. It's your story, after all. How can you describe a situation that once was imperfect five years ago as perfect now?

3. When you're done, thank yourself for having the courage to show up, massage wounds, and shower old places in your life with love, wisdom, and compassion.

FACING YOUR FEARS

We've talked throughout this book about fear and doing what scares you. Fear—of success, failure, the unknown, what others think—is a huge empowerment roadblock, but you don't have to let it freeze you. You can learn to face and manage fear, and doing so will boost your confidence and fuel the transformation process.

Everybody is afraid of something. Common fears include public speaking, flying, heights, bugs, snakes, strangers, success, blood/needles, and darkness. According to findings from a Chapman University Survey, 8.9 percent of Americans are afraid of zombies and 7.6 percent are afraid of clowns! In addition, the media fuels fear, keeping us glued to screens by broadcasting a continuous array of threats that "could" harm us or that we "should" be scared of.

Regulated by a small almond-shaped mass of gray matter in your brain called the *amygdala*, fear is a physiological response to danger. If you're trapped in a burning building, someone is holding a gun to your head, or you're being chased by a hungry tiger, that adrenaline rush triggered by the primitive reptilian part of your brain provides the energy necessary to get out of harm's way.

Here's the thing about fear: unless you're in immediate danger, fear is just a thought that triggers an uncomfortable emotion, which impacts your behavior. The problem is that fear narrows our attention and emotional bandwidth, tuning thoughts and feelings to the hazard frequency. Like a kink in a garden hose, this completely cuts off the Law of Attraction spigot.

Most fear is all in our head—a figment of our imagination. That's good news because while you can't always change your situation, you can overcome your fears by changing your thoughts.

If you want to live fully and make your next chapter your best chapter, you have to learn how to dance with fear, or as writer Elizabeth Gilbert puts it, tell fear to sit in the back seat of the car, rather than drive. The good news, to paraphrase American psychologist Karl Augustus Menninger, is fears are educated into us, and can, if we wish, be educated out.

ROCK YOUR MIDLIFE LAB

Transforming fear into courage

You can transform fear into courage using this three-step process adopted from the Mindful Self-compassion program as taught by Kristin Neff and Christopher Germer.

1. *Name it, you tame it.* First, acknowledge when you feel fear. When you tag fear, i.e., tell yourself, *This is just fear,* you bring the fear from the amygdala, the primitive reptile part of your brain, to the frontal cortex, where evolved executive function lives. This puts you in the driver's seat disabling fear and loosening its grip on you.

2. *Feel it, you heal it.* Notice how your body feels when you're in fear mode. Emotions are felt experiences in the body that can be physically released by relaxing your body, especially where you're holding fear. Fear is often felt as tightness in the chest, a racing heart, or stomach pain.

3. *Soften, soothe, and allow. Soften* the part of your body where you feel the fear. *Soothe* that part by placing a hand on it and perhaps gently massaging your body. Rather than pushing them away, *Allow* fear and other uncomfortable feelings to come and go.

Body-mind practices like yoga, tai chi, or meditation can also help you calm down when fear is trying to derail your dreams. The quickest way to generate peace is deep breathing. You'll fire up your parasympathetic nervous system, the rest-and-digest one, and calm down the fight-or-flight system. There are many breathing exercises you can try. For two great breathing techniques review Step 4.

Here's another tactic to try. Since fear and excitement are similar physiologically, try to reinterpret anxiety or fear signals as excitement. Your racing heart and sweaty palms are being generated because you are gearing up for a new adventure, not because you're scared. Think roller coaster ride where fear is fun.

Everything—happiness, joy, and that shiny, new life where you wake up excited to start your day—is on the other side of fear. So **F**ace **E**verything **A**nd **R**ise!

THE ONE YOU FEED

There's a Cherokee legend that says inside each of us are a pair of wolves, a good wolf and a bad wolf, each one fighting for domination. The good wolf represents joy, calm, love, peace, hope, abundance, compassion, generosity, kindness, and freedom—all the positive attributes that make us feel fabulous. It's the inner voice of truth that says *YES* to life's possibilities.

The other wolf is the exact opposite. This bad canine is the voice of scarcity, fear, self-doubt, self-loathing, insecurity, and envy. This wolf is ruled by our old reptilian brain that urges us to stay small and safe.

Which wolf wins? The one *you* feed.

Winning the inner battle between your good and bad wolves isn't easy. If you've spent years feeling defeated, desperate, and depressed, getting your good wolf to howl takes practice and patience. If being a *no* to your dreams is your default mode, saying yes can be uncomfortable.

However, you can be a *yes* to your life and become empowered using the techniques I've described. Start by refusing to feed the bad wolf. When she begs for food, slow down, take a few deep breaths, and remind yourself that you are safe and loved.

Remember that 99 percent of fear is in your head. Yes, be prudent and take all the necessary precautions to stay safe, but once you've done that, let the fear go.

Then work on being a *yes* in your life. Feed your good wolf a big bowl of self-love, self-care, and self-compassion kibble, and water her with gratitude. When she's satisfied, stand up, embody your "empowered star" self, and turn the page. It's time to get what you want and deserve from the relationships in your life.

CHAPTER SUMMARY:

- Empowerment is a process, which means you have to keep working at it. It involves becoming stronger and more confident, especially when it comes to controlling your life and claiming your rights.
- Being authentic (what you learned in Step 1) combined with the Law of Attraction will amp up your empowerment energy.
- You can overcome Imposter Syndrome by practicing mindfulness, lifting up others, and practicing self-compassion.
- Most fear is just *F*alse *E*vidence *A*ppearing *R*eal. You can use a number of techniques to face and overcome it.

8

STEP #6: REHAB YOUR
RELATIONSHIPS: FROM "WE" TO "ME"

*Whenever you're in conflict with someone, there is one
factor that can make the difference between damaging
your relationship and deepening it. That factor
is attitude.*

— William James

Warning: When you start to transform, some of your current relationships won't fit neatly into your new jigsaw puzzle of a life. As you show up authentically, amplify self-love, and bust out energized and empowered, some people may not like the new, clearer you. Like the unfurling dandelion in its snowy glory, you and your energy will be different. Congratulations—your new Me is emerging!

Now you want to be that new me, but what about all those other relationships in which you were a "we"? They don't fit anymore! How do you make the transition?

First, realize the most important relationship in your life is your relationship with yourself. Next, couple together the nurturing yin of self-compassion with the tough yang of self-compassion, that inner tiger that's there to protect, promote, and motivate you via the empowerment process (Step 5). This will provide the mojo you need in Step 6 to follow my Relationship Rehab Process, leading you to balance your relationships so that giving and receiving are more equitable and you feel more energized and fulfilled in all your relationships.

In this chapter, I will take you through each part of the process. But first, let's assess what it means to have healthy relationships in midlife.

RELATIONSHIPS AT MIDLIFE

After decades of living, we have many relationships—numerous connections with people, places, and things from partners, parents, and children to food, money, and our bodies. Some of these relationships are healthy and supportive. Others are sinking, unbalanced, and keep us stuck in reverse.

As Woody Allen puts it in *Annie Hall:* "A relationship, I think, is like a shark, you know? It has to constantly move forward or it dies. And I think what we got on our hands is a dead shark."

We're sandwiched between aging parents and growing children. Every day we encounter grumpy co-workers, needy friends, and an even needier spouse. And the kicker… we've caught the *disease to please*. As we unfurl the flamboyant spinnaker that's transporting us into our next chapter, stagnant relationships, like jagged rocks, threaten to ground us or tear a hole in our hull.

Be patient. Relationship Rehab takes time. The weekly yoga class, poetry reading, or much-needed spa retreat that you want to enjoy now may not jibe with old responsibilities like cooking dinner, watching your son's never-ending Lacrosse games, or attending the company picnic.

This is one of the hardest steps of next chapter creation. Once you learn to love yourself and press the empowerment button, it's all you can do to choke back the resentment and not scream *What about me!*

Scream! Swear! It's cathartic. The occasional F-bomb or curse can build emotional resilience and help you deal with situations in which you feel like you have no control. Research conducted by psychologists Richard Stephens and Claudia Umland at the University of Keele in Australia and published in *The Journal of Pain* found that moderate amounts of swearing can also reduce pain.

The desire to express, rather than stifle, your feelings is powerful and a good thing. It means your inner jungle tiger is hungry for new terrain. Rather than staying caged and busting your throat chakra, feed your inner wild cat. But please don't eat your loved ones. They still matter. Be courageous and take action to shift your relationship dynamics, and you'll find that the people who really love you also want to support you.

ROCK YOUR MIDLIFE LAB
The power of affirmations

Affirmations are positive statements that can help you feel stronger and overcome negative thoughts and self-sabotage. When used regularly, they can improve wellbeing and help reduce stress.

To use them, simply affirm a statement that you believe to be true throughout your day. You can also write the affirmation on Post-it notes and place them around your office and home. They will support you as you rehab your relationships, giving you the strength to shift dynamics and heal. Start with one of these affirmations:

- "I am safe and can speak my truth clearly, openly, and freely."
- "I am expressing myself clearly."
- "I have an important voice in the world that others listen to."

THE RELATIONSHIP REHAB PROCESS

My Relationship Rehab Process has three parts: 1) Let your Good Girl—the people pleaser who puts others before herself, wants everyone to like her, and avoids conflict at all costs—go; 2) Set healthy boundaries, and 3) Communicate powerfully so you *use* rather than *lose* your voice.

PROCESS #1: LET YOUR *GOOD GIRL* GO

My client Sara reminded me of how I felt when I played the part of the Good Girl, stayed small, and based decisions on what would make others, not *me,* happy. It was killing me and destroying my thyroid gland, which is located on the neck right below the Adam's apple by the throat chakra.

Here's what Sara shared shortly after we started working together:

"I'm an empath and good listener so people share a lot, which is exhausting. This has triggered throat issues, which are a combination of acid reflux, irritation, stress, and swallowing difficult emotions instead of speaking up." She went on: "I stay quiet even when I disagree with people because I was taught that silence is best and conflict is scary, and can permanently damage relationships. Sometimes, I waste hours playing with my phone to avoid speaking up. I tend to say yes to others (especially my husband) when I want to say no. I'm realizing that this is not the healthiest approach."

The good news is that things shifted quickly for Sara, and they can shift rapidly for you too. Using the techniques I share in this chapter, Sara became bolder and braver. She started to communicate her needs, wants, and desires and got her voice back. She realized that the people she loved wanted to support her and that ultimately she just needed to ask for help.

> *Nothing is perfect. Life is messy. Relationships*
> *are complex. Outcomes are uncertain.*
> *People are irrational.*
>
> —Hugh Mackay, psychologist and author

Holding emotional space for people who were only satellites in her life wasn't necessary. Rather than being a sponge for their draining problems, she referred them to human resources. The shift in her energy level and wellbeing was palatable. Instead of spending all her time taking care of others, she created space and time to care for herself. She started a daily yoga practice, spent time gardening, and took out the paints she bought when Covid started and actually used them.

Good Girl syndrome starts early and is rampant in our society. Like an ego eggshell, it protects us. However, that casing keeps us from breaking free and rebirthing ourselves so we can grow into something new. The relationship dynamics we have built up to keep the peace can feel so delicate like we're walking on eggshells. However, while the protective casing is easily broken, like the chick inside, relationships founded on love will survive and even thrive once the fragile shell is smashed. Yes, the process can be exhausting. Like a newly hatched chick, wet and tired from breaking out of its shell, you can revive yourself in the self-love incubator you built in Step 2.

We're not born with that ego shell. It is fashioned in our formative years and then embodied. We're taught to be good rather than strong, sensible rather than creative, perfect instead of innovative, and to fit in instead of standing out. Teachers and parents tell us: *Be a good girl, stay small, be quiet and neat, not needy, listen to your elders, don't do anything that might upset anyone, get good grades, and if you do fail, you didn't study or try hard enough …*

As children, we fear that if we don't listen to parents and teachers and do as we are told, we won't be loved and cared for. This fear of rejection causes us to internalize the voice of our early caregivers and shows up as the self-critic and the people pleaser. These voices mean well. They tell us what to do and how to act to keep us safe. The problem is that if we don't bust out and continue to listen to the voices, we will never chart our own course. Worse, we will die inside and leave the planet with regrets, having never shared our gifts.

As adults, Good Girl syndrome remains firmly in place. According to a study conducted by Stanford University, the most desirable adjectives to describe grown women were: *compassionate, warm, cheerful, soft-spoken,* and *loyal.* In contrast, desirable adjectives for men were *independent, assertive, dominant,* and *decisive.*

Research conducted by the *Harvard Business Review* found that only 7 percent of female MBA graduates negotiated their salaries during the job application process, compared to 57 percent of men.

No isn't part of your vocabulary because putting others first, as you smile and swallow your feelings, is what you were trained to do. Going out with girlfriends and letting your family fix their own damn dinner, telling your daughter to clean up her mess, or leaving work early to make that spin class… forget about it. That's selfish.

The *disease to please,* which manifests as the need to put others before yourself, is the leading issue I see with women at midlife who complain that they never have time for self-care.

One of my midlife clients, Lisa, a busy pastor for two churches, couldn't understand why she never had time to exercise and write her book. Out of shape and overweight, she knew how important exercise was for her physical and emotional wellbeing and even liked it. She also had a fantastic, impactful book idea, but instead of doing less for the church, she took on more work, performing double the hours that she was contracted for. Rather than delegating responsibility to church volunteers who were eager to help and saying no to her supervisor, she overextended herself.

In our work together, Lisa recognized her patterns. A recovering perfectionist and good girl, she was like Martha in the Gospel of Luke. In contrast to Mary who sat at Jesus's feet, Martha ran around "distracted by all the preparations that had to be made" and then felt hot and bothered, unappreciated, angry, and resentful when Jesus told her to chill and listen to his teachings.

Like Lisa, we midlife women long to care for ourselves and follow our hearts, but we have an immunity to change (as discussed in Chapter 2: Getting Unstuck) that we aren't aware of. Our unconscious belief is: *If I'm not available 24/7, I won't be loved or needed,* or *I'm the only person who can do this right.* Rather than scheduling Me time, we leave our schedule wide open so we can drive the kids to soccer practice, babysit the grandkids, chair the PTO bake sale, lead our team at work, or...

That's all about to change. In the previous steps, you've learned who you are and what you want. Now it's time to speak your truth and say no to others and yes to yourself. Misbehave! Let your inner Lillith out. Like Lillith, Adam's first wife, you may be scrutinized for being disobedient, but you're not ten years old anymore. You're a grown woman. No one is going to give you a time out or take away TV.

Don't worry if you're struggling with letting your Good Girl go and feeling guilty whenever you put yourself first. Despite all the 20th century feminist social movements—from suffragettes, some of who died for the right to vote, to the women's liberation movement in the 1960s and 70s—we haven't shed our dutiful membrane.

You've already started to break out by changing your beliefs about yourself and shifting the way you treat yourself. Now it's time to change your beliefs about how you're "supposed" to relate to others. Yes, like labor and delivery, it's uncomfortable, but it's what you must do to birth a new chapter.

Start by reviewing what you learned in Step 1 about knowing yourself. Forget about pleasing others and please yourself. Trying to be everyone's everything is a recipe for a codependency cake, frosted with frustration and resentment. Everyone is on his or her own journey. Each of us is responsible for our own happiness.

Then revisit Step 2: Befriend Yourself and own your self-worth. Know that you're always good enough. As poet Mary Oliver puts it in "Wild Geese,"

You do not have to be good.
You do not have to walk on your knees
For a hundred miles through the desert, repenting.

ROCK YOUR MIDLIFE LAB
Journal away your Good Girl

On this journey from *we to me,* let's start with a writing exercise. Pull out your journal or *Rock Your Midlife Playbook*[i], and ask yourself some deep questions about your Good Girl tendencies. Take your time with this exercise. Be honest with yourself and exam how unbalanced your relationships are. Here are some prompts to get you started:

- Do you feel that if people don't need you 24/7 you won't be wanted and loved?
- How is your Good Girl trying to protect or help you? Is she trying to keep you safe, look generous, avoid conflict, or not be rejected?
- Are you addicted to praise from others?
- What benefits are you getting out of always saying yes and over-giving?
- How does the over-giving make you feel?

- What would happen if you said *no* to others and *yes* to yourself more often?
- How would you like to be treated?
- How do you deal when other people are angry at you?
- When do you lose yourself replacing your wants, preferences, desires, dreams, and goals with making other people happy?
- Do you feel responsible for other people's feelings and have trouble expressing your own?
- Do you agree with others even when you really don't hold the same opinion?
- How often do you apologize?

Dealing with Conflict. The process of letting your Good Girl go and putting yourself first is hard and scary. Remember, your reptilian brain is hardwired for safety, not happiness. Your Good Girl and her sister, the people pleaser, have camped out with the lizard for years. Decades of unconscious habits designed to avoid danger have driven your behavior.

Breaking out of reptilian mode is possible. Shine an incubation light on your fears, and you'll crack your lizard shell and see they are *F*alse *E*vidence *A*ppearing *R*eal. Not only will you crack open and create space for something new to emerge, that illumination will help you see different options for your future.

With consistent attention to nurturing positive, neural pathways using practices mentioned throughout this book, such as self-compassion, gratitude, self-appreciation, and savoring the good, your lizard will scurry away, and you can keep reprograming your brain for happiness. You'll move your nervous system from the fight-or-flight response, which creates separation, to rest-and-restore mode, which helps you to connect with others. Even when their desires and opinions differ from yours, you'll find a way to relate peacefully.

Be warned: When you give your Good Girl a time out and stand up for yourself, she won't sit in the corner quietly. You will feel anxious and uncomfortable the first time you tell your husband you don't like the way he teases you, ask your teenager to clean up after herself, tell your boss you can't take on that new project, or let your mother-in-law know that you won't be making Sunday brunch.

Just Say No. Nein, nyet, non, nay... every language has a word that means *no* because it's so powerful. Learning when to say no is one of the most important things you can do to protect and promote yourself, and improve relationships. Along with sending a clear message to others, your no forces you to focus and prioritize. Use it often to delay, decline, delegate, deflect, and discuss issues, and you'll also feel more in control.

Yes, it's hard, especially for reforming people pleasers, so let's practice. Practice leads to imperfect, empowered action, so let's rehearse being the new you. Right now give yourself a supportive, surreptitious hug, and imagine standing up for yourself. Say the shortest, most powerful word in the dictionary out loud: No.

Here are some other sentences to try on:

No, I can't or won't do that.

No, it's not right for me.

No, I don't have time now.

Repeat this exercise again and again until your new me is ready for primetime.

To become an actualized adult and make your next chapter your best chapter, you have to stand up for yourself and stop avoiding conflict at all costs. Conflict is part of life and healthy relationships. When it's constructive and you use tools like boundary setting and Nonviolent Communications (which I'll teach you shortly), conflict can be good for relationships. It's a tremendous catalyst for change, brings out your strengths, and helps define and refine you.

Having a heated conversation about important matters in your life doesn't mean that you're not loved or the relationship is doomed. It means that you disagree and want your voice to be heard.

Ironically, not having conflict, especially if it entails stuffing your feelings and avoiding problems, can damage your mental (and even physical) health and your relationships. In contrast to stuffing or stifling, talking things out makes you feel better and determine the best course of action. Constructive conflict, where each party respects boundaries, builds trust, intimacy, and appreciation, can help your relationships grow and increase patience, love, and understanding. Knowing that you can argue and still care for each other in turn makes fighting less frightening.

Conversely, avoiding conflict has tremendous costs: your needs don't get met and you feel resentful and stuck. When you don't speak your truth and communicate with confidence, your throat chakra—which is the channel for expressing what's in your heart—becomes blocked and unbalanced. You hesitate and hide because you can't find your voice. You feel anxious and insecure rather than empowered and creative. When you're afraid to speak your mind, you may lash out and be critical of others.

There are two final things you need to do to let your Good Girl go: stop wanting everyone to like you, and don't take things personally. It's draining. What you believe about you is your business. What others think about you is theirs.

You can be like the dandelion. She doesn't stop growing because someone calls her a weed. She doesn't care because she knows that someday she'll be the stuff that wishes are made of. She's unstoppable and prolific, ready to scatter her seeds to the wind and be reborn.

ROCK YOUR MIDLIFE LAB
Rorschach test for relationships

One of my favorite techniques to stop taking things personally/needing to be liked, that double-edged sword that guides and protects your Good Girl, comes from psychologist Roger Covin, author of *The Need to Be Liked.*

Here's how to do it. Imagine you are an inkblot—one of those pictures that they show people during the Rorschach test. What others see about you (aka the inkblot) is about them, not you.

For example, one person may think your new silver hair is gorgeous because they are embracing their own natural hair color. Someone else may hate it because they are uncomfortable with aging or going dye-free. One person may view your new assertiveness as confidence. Another may feel you are being bossy.

As Don Miguel Ruiz explains in his book *The Four Agreements,* "Nothing people do is because of you. It is because of themselves. All people live in their own dream, in their own mind."

The Good Girl, the people pleaser, the desire to avoid conflict, the need to be liked, taking things personally… they are all characters and subplots in old stories that no longer fit who you are today. They're lampshades blocking your star and keeping you from sailing into your next chapter. As you remove them, you will be happier, more energized, and able to shine your light.

PROCESS #2: CREATE HEALTHY BOUNDARIES

Like Sara, we can feel simultaneously fed and fed-up with our relationships, longing for both connection and freedom. Shifting our toxic, moldy Good Girl *modus operandi* is tough. Just like you can't trim only the visible mold off your mozzarella to be safe (invisible mold spores harboring harmful bacteria such as listeria, salmonella, or E. coli can penetrate your cheese), you have to cut deep. You may need to throw some of your relationships away. As you're carving out a new life for yourself, you have to wield a major saber: *personal boundaries.*

Personal boundaries are the limits, guidelines, or rules of engagement you set for yourself within relationships. They are not walls of disconnection. Initiated from a place of self-love and self-respect, they are empowering and reinforce your right to personal space.

If people treat you poorly, it's because you don't love and respect yourself enough to set and reinforce boundaries. When your boundaries are poor, your solar plexus chakra, the energetic empowerment center becomes wobbly, and you feel drained.

Boundaries can be unilateral or collaborative; rigid, porous, or healthy. With unilateral boundaries, one person decides what is acceptable. With collaborative boundaries, acceptable behavior is mutually agreed upon.

Rigid boundaries create walls of disconnection, because you keep others at a distance as rejection protection. Common with people pleasers, porous boundaries are like cheesecloth. When this is your relationship fabric, you don't set hard limits because you fear rejection, have trouble saying no, and depend on validation from others.

Healthy boundaries identify both how you want to be treated *and* the consequences of crossing the line. Unlike rigid or porous boundaries, healthy boundaries arise from love, not fear. Generally, they also can be flexible, changing over time as situations and relationships shift. They empower you to value and voice your thoughts, feelings, and opinions. You can say no and can communicate your needs.

While establishing healthy boundaries can feel tough initially, there are huge benefits. Boundaries foster security, stability, predictability, and autonomy and protect you from being controlled. Mental health and self-care improve. You have more emotional energy and better relationships because you feel safe enough to open up and connect. As a result, self-confidence and self-esteem increase.

ROCK YOUR MIDLIFE LAB

Writing Your Personal Bill of Rights

The first step to create healthy boundaries is to write a Personal Bill of Rights. This is where you identify your physical, emotional, mental, and spiritual limits.

Pull out your journal or *Rock Your Midlife Playbook*[i]. It's time to activate your inner surveyor and make a list of what you are entitled to. These are your boundaries. When someone steps over the line, you can let them know and put them back in place.

Turn to a blank page and write on the top Personal Bill of Rights (PBR) or use the PBR page in your *Rock Your Midlife Playbook*[i]. Then write: *I have a right to...* and fill in everything you want.

Tap into your feelings. Give yourself permission to list what you and you alone (this isn't a democracy) are entitled to. Think about what you will and will not tolerate from family, friends, colleagues, and even strangers.

Your boundaries are informed by what is important to you, so review the list of core values that you created in

Step 1. Listen to your heart and gut, not just your head. Respect and love yourself enough to do this exercise.

Here are examples to get you started:

- I have a right to be happy.
- I have a right to express *all* my feelings, including difficult ones like anger, fear, and disappointment.
- I have a right to say no without feeling guilty.
- I have a right to personal space.
- I have the right to not know all the answers.
- I have the right to make my own decisions.
- I have a right to be treated respectfully.
- I have a right to be myself.
- I have a right to be by myself.
- I have a right to make mistakes and be imperfect.
- I have a right to be healthy and care for my body.
- I have the right to feel safe.
- I have the right to transform.
- I have a right to define my own needs, wants, and priorities.
- I have a right to prioritize my own needs.
- I have a right to accept failures and mistakes.
- I have a right to change my mind.
- I have a right to speak my mind.
- I have a right to make and follow my own values.

Take your time and continue to add to it as you become clearer about what you are entitled to. I highly recommend printing your PBR out and reading it daily until you become fully aware of your rights.

The next step is to list how you would like and deserve to be treated. This can follow closely from the first list. For example, *I would like to have others respect, prioritize, and listen to me.*

Enforce your boundaries. After you define your own rights and how you want others to treat you, it's time to figure out how you want to enforce your boundaries. This can be scary, especially if you aren't used to standing up for yourself. You may have to break old social contracts or refuse to be dragged into drama. Be prepared for others who were used to walking over you because you gave them permission, to be shocked or angry at the new you. Be patient with them! You allowed that disrespect by not enforcing or even setting boundaries.

Before you even start to enforce your boundaries, change your perspective. Get excited about saying yes to yourself and getting your needs met. Imagine having more love and support, and being able to do things you've always wanted to do without guilt. Let go of the old beliefs that you have about how enforcing boundaries means you're selfish. In their place, create new beliefs around the benefits of boundaries.

Now it's time to determine what the consequences will be when someone crosses the line. This will happen, so determine what you will do to enforce your boundaries. Specifics on how to do this are in Part III, Your 7-Day Plan.

If you have trouble determining your boundaries and being firm, don't hesitate to ask for support. Discuss the issue with a close friend or talk to a coach or therapist. Ask your spouse to support you especially when it comes to boundaries with other family members. Take work-related issues up with human resources.

Next communicate: Share the boundaries you've created with the people that are close to you. In addition, ask them what their boundaries are. Discuss what the consequences are if they cross the line. Which brings us to our next topic: Nonviolent Communication.

PROCESS #3: COMMUNICATE POWERFULLY WITH NONVIOLENT COMMUNICATION

Nonviolent communications (NVC for short) is a technique that is designed to increase empathy and help you to get your needs met. Based on the principles of nonviolence, it was developed in the 1960s and 1970s by clinical psychologist Marshall Rosenberg and has grown internationally through his Center for Nonviolent Communication. Used over time, the technique will improve the quality of your life and your relationships.

NVC is an antidote for miscommunication, which is why I teach it to all my clients and encourage them to use it on a regular basis. It's powerful because it replaces coercive, manipulative language that triggers fear, shame, and guilt and perpetuates conflict with language that evokes empathy, honesty, and connection. Plus, it's simple and easy to learn and use, and research shows that it's effective at conflict resolution and increasing empathy.

NVC has four components: *observation, feelings, needs,* and *requests.*

Observation means stating the specific facts—what you see, hear, or touch. Avoid judging and evaluating because the other person may feel criticized and react rather than respond.

Feelings involves sharing your emotions and sensations without going into thoughts and stories. The goal is to express yourself without criticizing or evaluating the situation or other person. Allow your feelings to reflect whether or not your needs are being met.

Next comes sharing your universal human *needs.* According to Rosenberg, they fall into seven categories: connection, physical wellbeing, honesty, play, peace, autonomy, and meaning. They are always positive and a variation of the categories.

Finally, you make a *request,* not a demand. The other person can say no and you remain open to hearing their thoughts. When making requests, keep your language clear, positive, and actionable.

Here's a sentence completion statement that makes the process easy:

When _____ (observation) happens, I feel _____. What I need is. _____ I'm asking you to _____ (request).

Here's an example of how to use NVC: The situation might be no matter how often you do the dishes, the kitchen is always a mess because your husband and kids don't clean up after themselves. Rather than doing the dishes yourself again, you can use NVC to talk with each family member. Here's how the conversation might go:

Observation: I'm noticing that the dishes in the sink are always piling up, and I always end up washing them.

Feelings: This makes me feel tired, angry, unsupported, and resentful. Need: I need support (part of the universal need for connection) and peace. Request: After you are done eating, can you please wash your dishes?

ROCK YOUR MIDLIFE LAB
Relationship inventory

Now that you've got a process for how to rehab your relationships, it's time to take an inventory of your current relationships and decide what you'd like to change. Take a deep breath. Looking at your relationships is hard, especially if you've been following the Good Girl script for years.

Grab your journal or *Rock Your Midlife Playbook*[i] and list the people you're in a relationship with: family members, friends, neighbors, co-workers, even your pets. This takes time, so keep a running list. Then evaluate what is working and what isn't. How do the people in your life make you feel? Do they respect you? A good way to evaluate your relationships is to list all of the violations you've experienced.

After you evaluate your relationships, you can determine which to put in rehab and which to delete. Not sure? Put a question mark by any relationship that needs shifting, but you're not sure exactly what to do. Relationship rehab and the journey from *me to we* is a constant work in progress.

FOUR KINDS OF RELATIONSHIPS

In this section, we'll look at the four kinds of relationships that present challenges in midlife: family relationships, grown and growing children, romantic relationships, and friendships.

Family Relationships. Because it's where the Good Girl eggshell forms, starting with family can be very rewarding. Blood may be thicker than water, but blood also clots from years of wounding. Those clots need to be removed, flushed, or dissolved.

The best way to get things flowing is through forgiveness, followed by discovering and meeting your unmet needs. Forgiveness doesn't mean you condone what was done. It means that you let the hurt and anger go so that you can heal and move on. Anger is toxic. As the Buddha is often quoted as saying, *Being angry is like drinking poison and expecting the other person to die.*

Parents and siblings somehow know how to push all of our buttons, yet at the same time, there is shared history, connection, and love. There's a lot of wisdom and growth in these relationships, and especially at midlife, lives become complicated and relationships naturally shift.

One of the many gifts of midlife is having an adult relationship with members of your family. These relationships are a great laboratory to let your Good Girl go, create boundaries, and use

NVC to get your needs met. Beneath all the tension run threads of love. Tap into it. Set an intention to give and receive love and respond, rather than react.

If you're blessed to still have your parents in your life, you can have a different relationship than you did as a kid. Forgive them and let childhood grudges go. See Mom and Dad as flawed human beings just like you. That's common humanity in action. Ask them about their lives and listen compassionately. There are clues here to help you know yourself.

My parents are in their nineties, and I treasure the times I spend with them, especially after Covid when I only saw them once in 2020, masked on a noisy balcony. We're all wiser and more real, vulnerable, and loving. Both my parents share pictures and stories of their younger days, and I enjoy these tales much more than I once did. There are no expectations and so much more presence and compassion. We can all sit together and savor happy memories, which creates connection and increases everyone's wellbeing.

If they haven't already, expect that the tables may shift, and you'll be the caregiver rather than the care receiver. Talk to your aging parents and determine where they are at financially and medically now and might be in the future. It's easier to change their living situation when things are stable than when an emergency, like a fall or stroke, occurs.

Be empathetic and compassionate, and use NVC to voice your concerns. Communicate with your siblings. Work together to come up with a list of options and create agreements in advance around who can help if Mom or Dad decline and need assistance.

Empty Nest. On the other side of the spectrum, you may have teenagers and are facing empty nest or you have adult children and/or grandchildren. Empty nest can be tough, but it's also an opportunity to redefine yourself and use that space to birth something new. Review Step 2. Practice self-compassion. Take time to deal with any difficult emotions, like uncertainty, grief, and sadness, that you may be experiencing. A chapter of your life is over, and your identity is shifting.

While parenting older children and being a grandparent can be fun and rewarding, it also can be draining physically, emotionally, and financially. Adult kids can go from thriving to struggling. They want us to be supportive and leave them alone. When you get that frantic phone call or text, do you let them sink or help them swim? No matter how old they get, our kids are part of us. It's all you can do to wish that they were toddlers again and you could hold them close and keep them safe.

If they live away from home, caring for and about them can be very challenging.

My kids are in their twenties, and I remember getting many frantic phone calls. There was the time my son got sick while working as a camp counselor. He had a slight fever in the morning, and the nurse let him climb Mount Mansfield (the highest peak in Vermont at 4,395 feet above sea level) on a 90-degree day. By the time he got back to camp, he was dehydrated, and his fever had spiked to 103. My ex and I had to debate whether or not to make a midnight run to pick him up or let the camp nurse take care of him.

That same summer my daughter was working on a food truck at music festivals. She went swimming, and while immersed in the water, thieves stole her tent and all of her belongings, leaving her with nothing but a towel and the bikini she was wearing. Her dad and I did our best to help her deal with the situation. Miraculously, all her belongings, tracked by her cellphone, reappeared by the side of a road some twenty miles away from her campsite.

Parenting young adults is a constant work in progress. Set boundaries! Respect, appreciate, and accept theirs. This is doubly important if you've got grandkids. Discuss rules and boundaries with their parents so you both are on the same page.

Welcome your adult children's significant others. These relationships are vital for their wellbeing. If you're in a new relationship yourself, give your kids space to get to know your partner. They may be adults, but in some ways, you have to treat them as if they were younger and ease into integrating your new partner into their life. Don't force things. New relationships take time to grow.

Keep doing the things that you and your kids love. Play board games. Go for a hike or bike ride. Share your wisdom when it's appropriate, but do it in a supportive rather than critical way. This will foster positive communication and enable them to come to you when they need help or advice. Working on parenting with your partner, if you have one, is also powerful, which brings us to…

Romantic relationships. Romantic relationships at midlife can be many things, from vibrant, sexy, joyful, meaningful, and pleasurable to dull, sexless, meaningless, and unpleasant. They also shift and change as you do. You may grow closer together or feel like you're miles apart.

Wherever you are on the primary partner spectrum, know that you have choices. You can enhance, reinvent, or leave your romantic relationship.

While our parents expected to stay together until death do us part, Splitsville is common and acceptable at midlife. Almost half of all marriages will end in divorce or separation, and Boomers have the highest divorce rate of any age group.

We're living longer and want our second adulthood partnership to be happy. In our twenties and thirties, we expect our partner to grow and change alongside us. At the half-century point, we may realize he's not about to change his ways and wonder: Do I really want to be with him for another thirty years?

You have so many options. Many people over fifty are living together rather than getting married. Others are staying married but living apart—aka LAT (living apart together). There's more potential than ever to rewrite rules, reinvent relationships, and find true love and happiness the second time around.

The balance of power, while it still needs more work, has started to shift for women. We're happily independent and don't need a relationship for security and definition. We're staying in marriages because we want to, not because we need or have to. We're craving intimacy, connection, and satisfying sex. If it's absent, we can work on our marriage or leave it. As issues like toxic masculinity and causes like the #MeToo movement surface, midlife men are shifting and wanting to raise their consciousness.

In working with hundreds of women at midlife, I've found that we fall into four categories: Happily committed, unhappily committed, happily single, or single and looking.

If you're happily committed, congratulations. Keep growing, having fun, and exploring life together. Prioritize quality time and find new projects from redoing the spare bedroom to playing Pickle Ball to share together. Stay curious. Travel. Socialize with other couples. You'll see your partner through fresh eyes.

Unhappily committed? Work on the relationship and prototype how splitting might look. Reintegrate date night into your week; spend time doing things that you both enjoyed and did when you first were together.

Reframe your partner's flaws. Wabi-sabi him, just like you Wabi-sabied yourself. Can you see underlying strength in his flaws or view them as charming? They are what make him unique and interesting. Ask yourself why his wrinkles irk you so much.

Midlife SEX

No conversation about midlife love would be complete without discussing sex. Sex at midlife, like so many things during this rich period of life, is up for redefinition. As relationship expert and author Esther Perel who wrote *Mating in Captivity: Unlocking Erotic Intelligence* is quoted as saying, "Sex changes—the expression of it, the energy of it, the rhythm of it, the acrobatics of it. But that doesn't mean the level of satisfaction has to decline. Sex can be just as satisfying, maybe even more satisfying, as we grow older."

Along with using plenty of lube, know yourself and your needs. In the years leading up to menopause, levels of the sex hormones estrogen, progesterone, and even the male hormone testosterone, are lower. As a result, moodiness and hot flashes may increase as libido decreases. Plus, you may have teenagers underfoot and be more concerned with getting a good night of sleep than having an orgasm.

On the positive side, as you reach your mid to late fifties, you hit menopause and empty nest, both of which can enhance your sex life. No kids plus no chance of pregnancy are major aphrodisiacs.

If the man in your life is having sexual dysfunction (The Massachusetts Male Aging Study found approximately 52 percent of men experience some form of erectile dysfunction), discuss it, and reassure him that you love him and that the condition is common and treatable. Encourage him to talk with his doctor to determine if there are lifestyle changes he can make and medications like Viagra he can take.

Don't treat sex as a performance with orgasm as the climax. Let go of expectations around when and how to "do it." Leave judgment outside the bedroom door. Much of what we learn about sex comes from pornography and impossible to emulate, media-driven standards that only exist in the movies. Focus on connection and giving and receiving pleasure. Have fun, experiment, and be curious. Expand your sexual menu by trying something new. Go away for the weekend. Pick each other up at a bar. Send sexy texts. Get a couple's massage. Buy sex toys. The most important sex organ is your brain. Use it.

If after trying to improve your relationship, you still want to end it, test the waters first before pulling the plug. Prototyping splitting can range from trial separation to talking to a divorce lawyer or friends who've gone through divorce.

Ending a long-term relationship is usually difficult, painful, expensive, and involves many different players. Fortunately, there are experts including mediators and divorce lawyers who specialize in facilitating a kinder, gentler divorce.

We are often taught that marriage is forever, but just like we may change careers, we may outgrow a partner and long to be with someone who is a better fit.

Don't stay in an unhappy union because of fear. Examine your fears. Are you worried about finances? Talk to a financial planner who specializes in divorce and create a post-divorce plan. Worried you'll be single forever if you leave? Check out personal ads or dating sites to get a sense of what's out there. There are wonderful people out there, and you can manifest a great relationship.

It's okay if you have no idea how to go about dating. Become the woman that you want to be (which is what this book is all about) and you will attract a partner who appreciates the new you.

YOU GOTTA HAVE FRIENDS

A huge blessing at midlife is having amazing friends. A study of 6,500 people published in the *Journal of Epidemiology and Community Health* found not having many girlfriends was associated with eroding psychological wellbeing.

While friendships matter at every age, at midlife, research shows that the quality of relationships rather than the quantity is what predicts higher levels of wellbeing.

Research shows that friendships have major benefits including increasing life satisfaction, psychological wellbeing, and overall health. The social support, compassion, and understanding friends provide can help you deal with depression, trauma, loneliness, and stress. Friendships combat loneliness and provide affection, companionship, and understanding.

That's the good news. The bad news is that at midlife, finding fabulous friends can be challenging. During high school and college, making friends is fairly easy and straightforward. Surrounded by people our age, it's easy to find friends with similar interests.

Fast forward a few decades, and you may not be exposed to a lot of potential candidates. There are work friends, but those relationships can be shallow, stressful, and not very fulfilling. You may talk about work even when you're trying to play, and may not have much in common outside of the office.

You may be so busy with work, raising kids, and marriage that you don't feel like you have the time to devote to friendships. If you want to have strong friendships, you have to prioritize these relationships and create space and time to cultivate them.

While it may not seem as easy as high school and college, there are numerous opportunities to make friends at midlife. If you still have kids in school, you can make mom friends. You may have different interests, perspectives, and beliefs, but you have the common bond of your kids. There's lots to talk about—the new principal, the innovative music teacher, dealing with your daughters' (and your) out-of-control hormones, or great restaurants in your town. Plus, there's easy proximity and shared space, from bake sales to soccer games, to hang out.

Another way to make friends is to follow a passion and do more things you enjoy. Take a weekly yoga, fitness, cooking, or painting class. Join a book group, sports team, or a spiritual community that resonates with you. Attend a community event such as a concert, fair, or farmer's market. Travel by yourself. Volunteer for an organization that you care about, or get politically involved. Make sure to schedule enough time afterward to hang out and chat.

Get to know your neighbors. Invite the couple next door over for a drink. Take a walk, smile, and say hi to the people you meet on the street. Pay it forward and buy the person behind you a beverage in your local coffee shop or bar. Adopt a pet. Research from the University of Western Australia found that strangers are more likely to approach people with pets than people walking solo.

You may also want to reconnect with friends you've lost touch with. Go to that high school or college reunion, or look them up on your favorite social media platform.

The beautiful thing about midlife relationships is that you get to decide who to spend time with and how you want to do it. As you change into the "new me," you have an infinite number of opportunities to find your tribe and create new besties that resonate with who you are now and who you are becoming. Drama doesn't have to show up. You get to connect with people who appreciate you and that you can be authentic around.

Whatever you choose to do to make new friends, release the stigma that meeting new people and putting yourself out there means you're sad or lonely. There are millions of midlife women who would be happy to be your friend, and you only need to find a few. Broaden your horizons and consider connecting with people that you may have once believed were outside of your social circle.

Remember, common humanity. We have so much in common and are all in this together.

In the often-quoted words of Ram Dass, "We are all leading each other home." In the next chapter, we'll explore spirituality and how you are in relationship with yourself, other people, and all that is. You are an essential part of an evolving world and a universe that is loving and expansive.

CHAPTER SUMMARY:

- To improve your relationships, you have to let your Good Girl and People Pleaser go.
- Good relationships require strong, healthy boundaries.
- Nonviolent Communication is a tested, powerful technique that can help you get what you want in relationships.
- Relationships change over time as you do. It's okay to move on and find new people as you transform.

9

STEP #7: ENLIGHTEN YOURSELF: FROM BOTTOMED OUT TO LIFTED UP

We do not need magic to transform our world. We carry all of the power we need inside ourselves already.

— J.K. Rowling

Congratulations! You've made it to Step 7, the final step you need to transform your life and make your next chapter your best chapter. This step is your spaceship to planet Spiritual Adventure. Strap in and get ready, because you're about to raise your vibe even higher and manifest what truly makes you (not your parents, your spouse, your kids, your boss) happy.

While this is my favorite step in my signature system, it isn't always a simple or easy one. I know it wasn't easy for me. It's taken me decades to break out of my shell and step fully out of the spiritual closet, but girl, has it been worth it. I now agree with the French philosopher, paleontologist, and Jesuit priest, Pierre Teilhard de Chardin who is often quoted as having said, "We are not human beings having a spiritual experience; we are spiritual beings having a human experience."

Wherever you're at in your relationship with God (or Spirit, Consciousness, the Divine, your higher power, or whatever you call what Lao Tzu refers to as "the eternal Tao that can't be named…"), sit with that statement from de Chardin for a moment. Let it roll around your self-concept. Acknowledge that you don't have to strive or be perfect to be spiritual. There's nothing you need to do because you already are a spiritual being. You can experience the Divine at any time. Simply sink into silence, feel into your heart, and you will radiate joy. Right here, right now, you can connect with the piece and peace of God that is inside you.

AWAKENING MY DIVINE SELF

Somehow I've always known this, but then I forget. Blame the spiritual amnesia on that Good Girl. When I'd approach the alter of my spiritual self, rather than sinking into quiet, eternal waves of peace, my *ego* would take over—"edging God out," a wordplay attributed to author and motivational speaker Wayne Dyer. Demanding to be heard and seen, she'd whip me into a people pleaser froth and set my spirit on sleep mode. The deep-rooted, "nothing is ever good enough," stressful stories would rage: *Work harder, make something of yourself,* drowning out that piece of God.

No matter how off track I got or how much I ignored my Divine essence, Spirit would gently tap me on the shoulder and remind me, *Darling, you are a soul. You are loved. You are loving. You are love.* Then I'd sink into that stillness, slow down, and let the richness of life guide me back to my essence.

I grew up in an academically-oriented, intellectual family where success was measured by accolades on a CV. Science was king, and anything that wreaked of woo was nonsense. God was an abstraction, rather than a moment-by-moment reality. In the 1960s and 1970s, the Reformed Jewish synagogue that I attended was more focused on social, political, and cultural issues than on God.

In my early twenties, before my celestial leap and lacking the secure structure of college and living alone in New York City, I became lost. The glamorous, corporate executive life I'd created with glitzy weekend rendezvous at nightclubs like Danceteria, where Madonna hung out, felt meaningless and empty. I didn't know how to find myself, let alone happiness.

Just like today, there was so much violence and suffering in the world —the Challenger Explosion, the AIDs Crisis, the Iran-Iraq War, the Bombing of Libya—nothing made sense. I didn't know what to do or how to deal. I had spent so many years in a Good Girl bubble, living to please others and following a societal success script that I didn't know what was right for me or how to cope with the international chaos that I read about every day in the *New York Times.*

To add to my depression, anxiety, and overall lack of hope and direction, I lost my job, leaving me anchorless. Disconnected from my intuition, I was traveling without a roadmap or GPS device.

Looking for guidance, I started to pray and read books from the Bible and Dante to Plato and George Gurdjieff. One evening drifting into sleep, I prayed for my muddy mood to disappear. The next morning, my Divine alarm clock went off. I woke up and the depression was gone! In its place was a single penetrating thought: I was here because God created me.

The simple concept shifted my reality. God, a personal God that I had never been introduced to, became very real. I prayed and thanked God for everything—frozen yogurt, short subway waits, new clients… Coincidences occurred constantly. I'd think of a person and they'd call, or a song and it would play. Or I'd open up a thick Manhattan phonebook and land on the business I was looking for.

I wanted to share my experiences and get guidance from people who had a personal relationship with God, so I started searching. Comfortable with my Jewish roots, I started my quest by consulting several rabbis. When I shared my experience, rather than helping me, they looked confused or alarmed. Where I came from, "I'm talking to God, and He's listening!" wasn't an exciting, enlightening experience. It was a statement that got you thrown into the loony bin.

Determined, I kept seeking and praying. On a bus bound for Cape Cod, a born-again Christian woman sat next to me. As we talked, she dropped "The Lord this" and "The Lord that" constantly and casually, like a wife mentioning her husband. Intrigued, I wanted what she had, but I was Jewish, and she was Christian. Surely the two were like oil and water and wouldn't mix.

Understanding my dilemma, she invited me to Jews for Jesus, an organization primarily funded by Christian donors that does a masterful job of marrying Jewish culture with Christian ideology. As they put it, *We exist to support you in exploring Jewish life with faith in Jesus.*

From the moment I walked through their downtown Manhattan door, which was four and a half blocks from my apartment, I was at ease and hooked. I "accepted Jesus as my Lord and savior," and eventually became a missionary myself. The organization moved me out to LA, where I spent several years converting Jews. While I didn't realize it at the time, I soon found the thick trappings of Judaism were a Messianic *yarmulke* that covered fundamentalist evangelicalism. Eventually, I left Jews for Jesus. My parents hired a deprogrammer who helped me see that I was being controlled. (Thank you, People Pleaser!). A few months later, I stopped following Jesus, but my heart retained the knowledge that God was personal and real.

A NEW AGE: CHRIST TO CRYSTALS

After letting go of fundamentalist Christianity, I gravitated toward the New Age Movement. Taking a break from learning the merits of fats, carbohydrates, and protein (I was working on a master's in nutrition at the time), I'd read about metaphysics, play with Tarot cards, and study personal transformation and healing. Then, just as my First Saturn Return was approaching—an astrological event that happens every 29.5 years and signals "time to get serious about your life," I met my ex, a devout atheist. Back into the closet, albeit with a little dabbling, I went.

Unicorn Books, a New Age bookstore housed in a lilac-colored Victorian about a mile from where I lived in Arlington, Massachusetts, became my new temple. I'd walk down the hill from our house, cross Massachusetts Ave, and enter a different world. Bells and wind chimes tinkled as you opened the door, and the smell of patchouli tickled your nose when you crossed the threshold. Rainbows, unicorns, crystals, and like-minded souls were everywhere. I felt safe and accepted.

The owners were friendly, suggesting books to read and classes from astrology to Zen to take. Curious, I signed up for something called Reiki. This was the early '90s before energy healing became popular and hospitals and hospice centers started offering Reiki to patients to reduce pain and enhance wellbeing.

The evening of class, I was given the first of two attunements (a ceremony that enables students to transmit Reiki) and the simple instruction: "Just do Reiki." Excited and a bit skeptical, I unleashed my new healing abilities on the closest human I could find, my husband at the time. I placed my hands on his doubting shoulders. Within seconds they started tingling and became warm and then hot for both of us.

While I resonated with Reiki and practiced on myself and family (my kids as toddlers tearfully begged me to apply it to their booboos), I hid my identity as a healer because I didn't feel safe to emerge from my spiritual closet. To mask my light, I accumulated degrees and certifications. I still cared too much about what others thought.

That changed the day I met Strawberry Jean, my first official hospice client. I became interested in hospice after caring for my mother-in-law, Anna, who was dying of lung cancer. Supporting Anna was a deeply moving, life-transforming experience that provided a safe space to explore my spirituality. I watched as she released all the trappings of the world. She stopped drinking coffee and ended her daily standing date with Oprah. After getting her affairs in order, she stopped wearing glasses and false teeth.

Like a mother giving birth, she was dilating. As she let go of the world, her spirit got brighter and a new level of authentic energy emerged. At times she could be trying—like a 180-pound toddler who wanted to go outside one minute and inside the next—but it was an honor to be in her presence during her final days. I let go of time for the weeks I was with her. I became more mindful and patient. I followed the words of my Reiki Master: "Just do Reiki."

After Anna passed, I felt called to do hospice work. Being close to death wakes you up and reminds you that you are running out of time. Off to volunteer I went, which is how I met Strawberry Jean.

Jean was resting peacefully when I arrived at the nursing home where she was living. Everything about her was gray—her craggily face, sparse hair, and sunken eyes. Clearly she had lived a hard life. Confused and frail, she complained of fatigue and requested something to drink. She sipped ice-cold milk and talked about her childhood on the Islands of Vermont, where I live now, riding horses and making strawberry ice cream from berries that grew on her family's farm.

As she talked, I gently placed my hands on her shoulders and started doing Reiki.

Clearly enjoying the experience, she said emphatically, "Don't take your hands off my shoulders." In that moment, as the healing energy flowed through my body, I was overwhelmed with love for this dying woman who was a complete stranger. Through moist eyes of compassion, I saw, rather than a shriveled, old woman, a beautiful being.

"I think you're wonderful," I said.

"No one's ever said that to me," she replied.

Blessings and spiritual direction often come in strange packages.

OUT OF THE CLOSET

The experience of sharing Reiki with Strawberry Jean kicked me out of the spiritual closet. It was time to unleash my inner healer. I decided to teach Reiki at a local yoga studio and share distant Reiki healing virtually in my Facebook group, *Dr. Ellen's Mastermind.*

Here's what I discovered: when you embrace your unique spiritual gifts and courageously show up as your true, authentic self, it becomes easier for others to find you and for you to create a life that is aligned with your soul.

The universe applauded my decision to leap out of the closet by blessing me with three miracles. First, the class sold out. Eighteen people signed up, surpassing the limit of 15. I was terrified that I wouldn't do the attunements correctly. However, not only did all thirty-six hands light up with Reiki energy as my students practiced, everyone wanted to continue to study with me.

Miracle number two happened as I was performing the first Reiki attunement. Joe, one of the students, had a nasty cut on his thumb from a misguided vegetable-chopping incident. A thick, bloody bandage swaddled the deep, oozing wound. During the first of two attunement ceremonies, as I was holding Joe's hands, the same intense, compassion that I'd experienced with Strawberry Jean hit me. After class, Joe took off the bandage and showed me that his thumb had completely healed. There was a small indent in the skin showing where he had cut himself, but no scar.

When I arrived home, energized by my class, there was an email from an editor of *Touch Magazine.* The European magazine features Reiki masters and practitioners, and they wanted to interview me

There was no turning back and nothing to be afraid of. I would find a way to combine my intellectual, academic side with my healing gifts. So here I am, sharing years of conventional training as a psychologist, coach, and nutritionist, guiding and inspiring you in this book. Each breadcrumb on my life's journey has brought me to this moment. Your life has done the same for you.

As you build your spiritual spaceship, remember the times in your life when you felt lit up. Like for me, it was Reiki and hospice, you have spiritual breadcrumbs that have already appeared to light your way. Let them guide you to what's next. You don't need to know the way home. We never do, because Spirit only reveals the foot or handhold needed to reach the next summit.

TURNING ON THE SPIRITUAL SPIGOT
AND WATERING YOUR SOUL

Something interesting and infinitely wonderful happens spiritually at midlife, if you let it. Knowing there is no knight in shining armor and nothing to save you, you learn to save yourself. You mend your own damn life, and you do it now because you're running out of time.

Mending happens from the inside out. Rather than changing your external reality (moving to a new town, getting a different job, having a facelift, losing weight or…) hoping it will make you happy, you focus on your inner self. When a new job or relationship do show up, it's because you changed on the inside and attracted something better suited to the new you. And the weight loss? When your soul is in alignment, you won't want to have a threesome with Ben and Jerry. The facelift? You'll prefer your unique wrinkles etched from years of wisdom to being defaced.

As you make friends and explore the Source of all Life, you'll naturally water your soul and blossom into the individual that you were meant to be. Maybe you're a rose, perhaps a pansy, tulip, a sunflower, bromeliad, or a dandelion who, when things fall apart, plants seeds and grows again.

Like your soul, each flower needs a different milieu. Roses thrive in direct sunlight and neutral soil. Pansies prefer morning sun and slightly acidic soil. Dandelions are resilient gals who grow wherever they are planted, busting through cement or blacktop.

As you connect with what ignites your spirit, relax and realize that you have everything you need to succeed and you can't do it wrong. You don't have to copy anyone else because this is your path. The JOurneY isn't about being more like Jesus, Mary, Joseph, Buddha, or Mother Theresa. It's about being the you-est you.

Take a moment and appreciate how marvelous you are. Forget all the BS crap you were told—stay small, be humble, don't shine. In the words of Marianne Williamson, author of *Return to Love*, "Your playing small doesn't serve the world. There is nothing enlightened about shrinking so that other people won't feel insecure around you." Be mindful of and grateful for your good qualities. Blossoming fully doesn't mean that you're superior, and it won't alienate you from others. Remember, everyone else has good qualities too. That's *common humanity*. When you shine, you give others permission to do the same.

ROCK YOUR MIDLIFE LAB
Creating a spiritual practice

Having a regular spiritual practice—activities that center you and help you find purpose and meaning—will feed your spirit and boost your overall wellbeing. You'll be calmer, more peaceful, and present, and the fabric of your life will feel different— more like cotton or silk than acrylic or polyester.

You don't have to spend a ton of time on your spiritual practice. Keep it simple. Less is more. Intention (what you intend to do each day) and consistency are what are key. Experiment. Put out the Do Not Disturb sign for inner and outer critics, and inner peace will show up. Know that there's no right way to do it. It's helpful to start your day with a morning practice and then have other touchstones throughout the day that ground and re-center you.

Personally, here's what I do: When I first wake up, I tune my mind to Station Positivity by thinking about how wonderful my life is and setting an intention that today will be the best day of my life. As my feet touch ground, I thank God for my life. After the basic bathroom stuff is done, I do *The 5 Tibetans*, a series of exercises designed to wake up your chakras and enhance longevity (see Resources Section at the end of the book). I meditate for five to twenty minutes while practicing self-Reiki and self-compassion. I may pick a Tarot card, read something inspirational, and/or journal. All in all, the whole process takes about thirty minutes.

Along with meditation, prayer, journaling, gratitude, and using affirmations, here are other things you can do as part of your spiritual practice.

- Bless and drink plenty of water. I sometimes put Post-it notes with positive words like *energized, happy,* or *joyful* on my water glass and bless the contents prior to drinking.
- Spend time in nature. You are part of nature. Walking outside among the trees (*sans* phone, of course) and taking in all the sights and smells you encounter will renew your soul. This is actually a Japanese practice called *shinrin-yoku*, translated as "forest bathing," or walking in the forest using all your senses.
- Unplug from all media for a day or an hour.
- Sink into silence and stillness. You just might

notice that Spirit has been talking to you all along.

- Ground and center yourself. Walk barefoot outside and sense the grass on the soles of your feet. Or imagine that there is a cord running from the base of your spine to the center of the earth, grounding you like the roots of a giant tree.
- Get sensual. Experiment with essential oils or light incense. Arrange flowers. Listen to beautiful music. Cuddle a pet or someone you love.
- Find a body-mind practice you like, such as yoga, tai chi, or chi gong.

At midlife, turning on your spiritual spigot becomes less about seeking and striving, and more about landing exactly where you are. You let go of the old Good Girl stories about who you are supposed to be and embrace being where and who you are and how life is today. That's *mindfulness,* experiencing what you're experiencing in the eternal now, this moment, which is all there is.

Yes, I've mentioned mindfulness previously, but it's so important that I'm going to discuss it again. Along with self-compassion, mindfulness is one of the most powerful practices to tote in your next chapter Spiritual Toolkit. Mindfulness enables you to gain an undistorted, clear perspective on your life. Rather than getting lost in rumination, worry, and regret, which generates anxiety, stress, and depression, you accept yourself and your life as it is.

Mindfulness is your get out of "I'm not good enough" jail free card. It's your permission slip to forgive yourself and let the heavy shit go. Like self-compassion, mindfulness is a muscle that grows with use and fosters self-awareness and gratitude. Instead of whining and complaining, practicing mindfulness provides the conscious connection to observe your situation. Even if you don't like something, you'll see that in this moment you are safe and have the resources and resilience to handle whatever life tosses your way. Practiced by successful people including Oprah, Arianna Huffington, and Bill Gates, mindfulness is a superpower.

> *"Mindfulness allows you to experience your life in the present without ruminating about what just happened, what should have happened, what almost happened. It is the ability to pay attention to what actually matters."*
>
> —Sam Harris

Not sure what to do? You can *always* take a deep, mindful breath to calm down and find something to be grateful for. Doing this will shift your perspective and elevate your vibration so you see solutions rather than problems. Within every crisis there is opportunity.

ROCK YOUR MIDLIFE LAB
Meditate, please don't wait

Take one deep breath and savor the sensation of breathing. Now take another and experience being in your body. Take a third and smile. How do you feel?

Congratulations—you just meditated! That's all there is to it. Breathing—linking one breath with another and another—is the essence of meditation. You don't need to ship off to India or find a guru. Simply being present with yourself for a few minutes a day can make a huge difference in your life.

The research shows meditation changes key parts of your brain for the better. It helps preserve the entire brain as you age and increases cortical thickness in the hippocampus, a part of the brain that governs learning and memory, and other areas involved in regulating emotions. As mentioned before, it helps deactivate the Default Mode Network (DMN) or "Me Center" of the brain, reducing that chattering "monkey-mind" that keeps you up at night. Regular practice can help increase self-awareness and reduce anxiety, pain, worry, and depression.

There are many types of meditation. You can choose to focus on your breathing or anchor your awareness on an object, such as a flickering candle or flower. You can repeat a word, such as *peace* or *love*, or send compassion to yourself or others.

Keep at it. Over time meditation will increase mindfulness and help you become more aware of your thoughts—the good, bad, and neutral. You'll start to notice and stop believing and fueling old stories that keep you stuck. You'll see thoughts are mental energy that you can feed or starve. You can hold on to the positive ones and let those that aren't serving you go. Over time, difficult thoughts will become less sticky, and you will experience more joy and less angst.

YOU ARE THE ANGEL IN THE MARBLE

Right here, right now you can enjoy being a soul having a messy, human experience. Like a Michelangelo sculpture, you are the angel in the marble being carved, ready to be set free. The messes, the challenges, the moments of sadness or confusion—these are tools that are chipping away dross to reveal your soul. The big challenges help you understand who you have become and what you need to change. Each swipe of the cosmic chisel is an opportunity to swap anger for love, greed for generosity, or fear for faith.

"When you realize that suffering and discomfort are the call to inquiry you may actually begin to look forward to uncomfortable feelings. You may even experience them as friends coming to show you what you have not yet investigated thoroughly enough."

—Byron Katie

While nobody wants or welcomes difficulties, they are inevitable. It's *common humanity*. When you have the soul perspective, you see silver linings. You grow like King David who prayed in Psalm 139: "Search me, God, and know my heart; test me and know my anxious thoughts. See if there is any offensive way in me, and lead me in the way everlasting."

You're older, wiser, and more willing to be vulnerable, which is the key to what researcher Brené Brown calls "wholehearted living." You have the strength and inner awareness to be yourself. Rather than ego-driven success, you focus on love (for self and others) and what makes you happy. There is a deeper understanding that you are part of the circle of all things. This enables you to feel connected and a part of all that is.

The fear that you are running out of time and have a mission outweighs the other fears: fear of success, failure, and what others will think. *What am I here to do?* and *How can I be of service?* are the questions you start to ask.

The years 2020 and 2021 clearly showed that the world is a mess. Covid illuminated the shadows and revealed all the cracks, inequalities, and inadequacies. The greed and cruelty that have caused tremendous suffering for humanity and the planet for centuries surfaced and were in our face beneath the masks we were forced to wear.

This mess affects every person on the planet. It's the Butterfly Effect. Forest fires in California and Turkey impact the air in New York City as well as the food that reaches your grocery store. That's the bad news. The good news is that you can be part of the cleanup crew. Know that you are here for a reason and that you can make a difference and help repair the world.

Wise, loving midlife woman—your kids, grandkids, great-grandkids, and beyond are depending on you. You don't have to save the world, just a piece of it. Work in a soup kitchen. Walk the Appalachian Trail and raise money to conserve it. Pick up trash or bike to work. Teach 3rd graders with learning disabilities how to read. Write a book about how you got through recovery, cancer, or divorce, and let your pain be someone else's medicine.

Being of service will fuel your spiritual spaceship into the stratosphere of love.

With each act of service, you'll create ripples of connection and meaning. You'll increase your own wellbeing and the wellbeing of others. Find a cause that you care about or a problem that you want to help solve. Be creative in your approach by connecting with the Divine. The options for contributing are endless, and giving back doesn't even have to take a lot of time or money.

In 2009, at the Vancouver Peace Summit, the Dalai Lama said, "The world will be saved by Western women." Now it's time for midlife women to strap on their capes and be the superheroines that we're capable of being, and come to the rescue.

Visualize a different world and believe in miracles. The word *miracle* comes from Latin *miraculum,* meaning "a wondrous work of God." That is what you are.

Everything—the fact that you are alive at all, perhaps sipping tea, reading this book—is a miracle. When you get that at midlife, really comprehend what an incredible wonder life is, you can rock midlife too.

This sets you free to be a curious explorer, digging up old dirt and recycling or repurposing it, planting new seeds, simultaneously being and becoming. As T.S. Eliot wrote in his famous poem "Little Gidding":

> *We shall not cease from exploration,*
> *And the end of all our exploring*
> *Will be to arrive where we started,*
> *And know the place for the first time.*

A FINAL REMINDER

All the materials for the new life you are creating through your spiritual enlightenment are already within you. Plant yourself where you are most needed. Water yourself with love. Shed your own seed coat by removing all the barriers that keep you from blossoming. Take in the sunlight and share your fragrance with the world. Then like the resilient, nutritious, and prolific dandelion, spread seeds. Water them so they spring to life. Ditch the old belief systems, thoughts, habits, and patterns that have hidden your authentic self. They are like light-blocking window shades, keeping you in the dark and preventing the photosynthesis you need to grow and glow.

As you feel more connected to both your roots and the light, you can remove the heavy fabric, that bearskin rug that's been keeping you comfortably uncomfortable, and let your own light shine brightly, nakedly, brilliantly. You can be like the dandelion, able to thrive anywhere you are planted, basking in your snowy glory, and granting wishes to anyone, including yourself.

CHAPTER SUMMARY:

- You are a human having a spiritual experience.
- You already have everything inside of you to connect with and express your Divine self. At midlife, spirituality is less about seeking and more about landing where you are.
- Creating a regular spiritual practice can help you be calmer, more peaceful, and present.
- Everything, including you, is a miracle.

10

CONCLUSION:
FINESSING THE PHOENIX:
LEARNING TO SURF THE WAVES
OF CHANGE

I live on an island between surf and turf. Toward the west lies my watery playground, Lake Champlain. This great, but not quite "Great Lake," is home to 318 species of birds, eighty-one types of fish, and more mosquitos than you can shake a swatter at. During summer, I swim, kayak, fish, and sail. Come January, when the silky water turns hard, I ski and walk on ice frozen two feet deep. Most evenings, I'm blessed with glorious lakeside sunsets. Depending on the season, between four and nine, the sky slowly morphs from blue and white to a kaleidoscope of lower chakra hues of red, orange, and yellow.

Round the back of my house, to the east lies a classic Vermont dairy barn. The cows provide manure for our *ginormous* vegetable garden that's really more of a farm, overflowing with rows of greens (kale, collards, bok choy, mustard, and Swiss Chard), six types of tomatoes, including a hybrid called Pink Boy purchased at our local farmers' market, and green and red cabbage destined to be spun into sauerkraut. The squash patch—home to zucchini, butternut, summer, and spaghetti—is out of control, only eclipsed by the Great Pumpkin which is bigger than Rosie, my border collie.

I feel like I'm living in a Mary Oliver poem. The first time I drove up to this ten-acre property in my little, red Ford C-Max past hundreds of rows of elephant-eye-high corn, the theme song from *Gone With The Wind* played in my mind. The property's former owner was a florist, and every day there's a new bloom to swoon over—white and pink peonies the size of baseballs, smiling tiger lilies, and deep purple Italian Clematis that are home to a nesting dove and her two chicks.

To quote something Oprah once said, "When I look into the future, it's so bright it burns my eyes."

Four years ago, if you had told me I'd be this happy, living on a romantic island with an Aquarius man who is one part master gardener, one part high tech guy, one part yogi, and 110 percent lovable, I would've screamed, *Sign me up!*

Problem was, back then, I was 100 percent married, caught in a negative-vibe depression spiral, and too scared to break free.

SO CLOSE, AND YET ....

Ironically, in the summer of 2017, I was two miles and yet a million light-years away from my current surf and turf paradise. While back then I longed for a different life, I had no idea what my future held because, as Paul wrote in First Corinthians, "The mind cannot conceive of the things God has prepared for you."

That summer, my then husband and I were dropping off our youngest, Marcus, at YMCA Camp Abnaki, which is on the island of North Hero in Lake Champlain, where I now live. Marcus was going to be a Counselor in Training for six weeks, and we were going to be empty nesters for the first time in twenty years. Excited and a little sad, I kissed my son goodbye, and off we went.

I was hoping the six weeks *sans* kids—my daughter was working away from home most of the summer as well—would repair and reignite romance, and our relationship. The summer was a bust rather than a blast. Like a set of once shiny teeth rusted by years of soft drinks and grinding, things continued to erode.

We fought; we squabbled; he yelled at me. I became traumatized, resentful, and withdrew. The pattern repeated again and again, like a tragic version of *Groundhog Day*. I couldn't see myself spending my one, wild, precious life, my second adulthood with this man. We were on different trajectories. I wanted to rock midlife—to live authentically, with passion, and have adventures. He wanted to sit in a rocking chair, drink scotch, and watch the History Channel.

After my friend Cynthia died of cancer, everything changed. Life felt so dear, so short. The caged tiger craved freedom. I wanted out ASAP, but ending an almost twenty-five-year marriage I knew would be messy, unpleasant, cutting, hurtful. There aren't enough words to describe how truly difficult it would be. I resonated with Bono singing, "With or Without You."

I started fantasizing, daydreaming about what it would be like to be in love with someone else. During a coach training the spring before I left my ex, we created a bucket list entitled "25 things I Want to Do Before I Die." Between *have more deep friendships* and *go kayaking was number seventeen: Have another romantic relationship that resonates with who I am and who I am becoming.* Be careful what you wish for.

That summer, I watched the movie *Eat, Pray, Love* alone. The bestselling biographical book, that became a hit movie, by Elizabeth Gilbert, tells the story of how Gilbert discovered herself after divorce and found love again. Towards the end of the movie—the Love part— there's a scene where Filipe (played by the hot, sexy Javier Bardem) smiles and says to Elizabeth Gilbert (played by Julia

Roberts), "Darling, it's time." Soft, sexy Latin music plays in the background. Filipe takes Liz by the hand and they dance into the bedroom. I swooned. The scene jolted my heart like an EKG machine. Like a hungry tiger, I craved being in love.

HARNESSING THE LOA

Little did I know that I was performing magic, harnessing the Law of Attraction (LOA) to magnetize and create a new vibe that would change my trajectory and transform my life forever. The secret to using the LOA isn't actually a secret. People have known for centuries how to do it.

To review what you learned in Step 5: Empower Yourself, there are three simple phases: 1) ask, 2) believe, and 3) receive. You ask for what you want, believe you can have it and are open to receiving it.

What is the key to using the LOA to rock your midlife?

First, you have to know what to ask for. This is why Step 1: Knowing yourself, is so important. If you want to be happy, you have to know yourself well enough to ask for the right things.

Second, you have to keep the faith that what you want is coming. This is where Step 7: Enlighten Yourself is key. Whatever you call "it"—God, Spirit, Consciousness— you have to have a relationship with and believe in a higher power, an energy that is working for your highest good. You have to feel into your future by visualizing the outcome—seeing, hearing, tasting, feeling, smelling—experiencing it vividly as if it's happening to you. Believing it so deeply that you can say thank you before your heart's desire has even arrived.

Third, you have to feel worthy enough to receive. This is where Step 2 comes in. You must love yourself enough to feel worthy of receiving what you truly want. So often I meet women at midlife who know what they want, but they have such low self-worth that subconsciously they are channeling: I don't deserve this. They've put a ceiling on their happiness, so instead of creating and welcoming positive change, they sabotage themselves. Don't let that be you.

In addition to those three phases, it helps to rock Step 5: Empower Yourself by rallying courage. You have to be hungry enough to face your fears and follow your heart. You must gather the guts to step out of your comfort zone and transform your inner Cowardly Lion into a fierce tiger. As Glennon Doyle shares in her brilliant book *Untamed,* you have to stop being a domesticated big cat chasing dirty, pink bunnies. You have to realize, as she wrote in her book: "You are not crazy. You are a G-D cheetah!"

UNLEASHING MY INNER TIGER

Have you ever wondered why you are attracted to certain animals? These members of the natural world are your power animals transmitting information to your soul. They actually choose you. Pay attention and get to know them. They have gifts to share and will help you know yourself and navigate midlife with more ease and authenticity.

I am a tiger. I was born in 1962, the year of the Fire Tiger, and have always been fascinated by these fierce creatures. Like tigers, I'm strong, sensual, fierce, impulsive (oops), resilient, and confident. I love adventure and freedom, and I know the best way to overcome obstacles and fears is to stay calm and in my place of power.

However, for years I acted more like a dog than a powerful cat, endlessly trying to appease and please others. While few animals dare to challenge tigers, who are at the top of the food chain, I felt controlled and criticized on a daily basis by my ex whose power animal is the monkey. (Tigers are uncomfortable and annoyed by monkeys.) My stifling, unfulfilling marriage left me drained and miserable, rather than passionate and hungry for life.

Ironically, the midlife women I coached were soaring while my life was pancake flat. I felt inauthentic and dead inside. I longed to live up to my true potential but was too scared to take the tiger by the tail and face my fears.

As my Second Saturn Return approached, my soul was urging me to get back on track and get to my life's work, which is inspiring you to love and accept yourself and start rocking your midlife.

It was time to get real and face the fact that I was comfortably uncomfortable, and needed to change. Once I accepted that, the internal and external resources I needed to get unstuck appeared. They were actually there all along—friends, family, clients, co-workers, and therapists had been encouraging me to leave my ex for years, but I needed to get to a breaking point before baring my teeth, flexing my claws, and unleashing my inner tiger.

Four years ago, like a phoenix (who along with tigers are one of the four sacred animals of Chinese mythology), I blew up and burnt down my life. From the ashes of my Good Girl people-pleaser archetype rose what Kristin Neff calls *fierce self-compassion*, promoting, protecting, and motivating me towards something new and exciting.

I went tiger on a Sunday in October 2017. My son, ex, and I were watching the movie, *Baby Driver*. Two butterflied chickens that I had spent an hour preparing were roasting in the oven. It was late, and the salivating inducing aroma of the twin birds was triggering overwhelming hunger.

We paused the movie and headed into the kitchen. As my ex carved the birds, I reached over and grabbed a back to nibble because I was starving.

He screamed, "How dare you eat while I'm working here!" "Fuck you," I replied and walked out the door.

Enough was enough. That bite of chicken back was the dromedary straw. Years of suppressed anger and submerged pain shot to the surface, a tsunami shipwreck ready for salvation. Steam still rising from my risen battleship, I slammed the door on my old life, gritted my teeth as I faced divorce, and moved forward!

HOW DID I GET HERE?

Essentially, I followed the seven steps that you have in your hands. It's a formula that works. Follow it and you will learn to know and love yourself. You will have the energy, clarity of mind, empowerment mojo, supportive relationships, and Divine support to break free from whatever is holding you back, so you can rock your midlife too. Most important, you will figure out what makes *you*—not your spouse, your boss, your kids, your parents, siblings—*happy*.

However, you don't have to blow up your life the way I did—although you can. You can take a gentler, slower approach if you prefer. Think of transforming your life like learning French. You can learn a couple of words a day and build your vocabulary gradually. Or you can book a one-way ticket to Paris and immerse yourself in *Je ne sais quoi,* vowing not to leave until you can order dinner and have a good argumentative discussion with the natives about religion, food, or politics while sipping Bordeaux.

The decision, like all decisions in your life, is up to you. However, some radical changes will be necessary if you want to live in integrity rather than duality. If you want to rock your midlife, rather than staying stuck and conforming, you will have to connect with and speak your truth, honor yourself, and live with integrity. If you're in duality, which means you are not acting in accordance with your true self, you may have to burn some bridges and belief systems to have a clean slate to create something new that *is* in alignment with your soul. The reward is that you will discover greater happiness and clarity of purpose. You will be wiser, more present, and guided from a place within that keeps you moving forward. When demons—negativity, impatience, the People Pleaser, doubt, anger—do show up, having learned your lessons you will shake them off and stay on track. If you do stray from your path, which will happen, your soul will tell you how to get back to your true North.

You can also start with any of the 7 Steps presented so far or work on several at a time. Or go straight to my 7-Day Plan that follows in Part III to jumpstart your midlife transformation with a day-by-day plan that has you taking baby steps in each of the action areas.

Personally, I started with Step 2: Befriending Yourself. Learning to love, respect, and honor yourself changes everything. Self-love and self-compassion fuel the inner fire that will give you the courage to take a hard look at your life and feel empowered enough to make changes. You'll take care of yourself and be energized from a place of self-love rather than self-loathing. When you truly love yourself, you'll stop doing things that insult your soul. Permission to feel good will appear, and feeling good will become your North Star.

DESTINATION VIBRATION

Like a star waiting to be born, I had many miss-takes and hurdles along the way to my surf and turf paradise. Those three years of transformation felt like I was climbing the Himalayas without a Sherpa.

The final energetic shift that changed everything and brought me to this magical surf and turf paradise was an exercise called Destination Vibration, or DV for short. This powerful technique showed up in my life the moment I needed it most, in March of 2020 when everything shut down due to the COVID-19 pandemic.

That spring I was getting ready to break out big time. I was breaking up with Rebound Guy and moving out to a new apartment. My bags were packed and the movers were booked. Then Covid hit, and I traded freedom for lockdown.

To cope with the isolation, insanity, and uncertainty, each Thursday evening I gathered via Zoom with a group of women seeking trans-formation. Together we engaged in a number of alchemical exercises, including one called Destination Vibration.

The practice was simple: think of a time in your life when you felt good—happy, free, authentic, joyful—and visualize it as vividly as possible several times a day. So every day, numerous times a day (we were in lockdown after all, and there wasn't a ton to do) I saw myself engaging in one of my favorite activities: dancing. There I was at age five, doing dizzying pirouettes; in second grade, wearing a black leotard, tights, and tutu, leaping across the stage as the school chorus sang Cat Steven's "Morning Has Broken"; at fourteen, gracefully competing in gymnastics floor-ex; at twenty-seven, circle dancing at a Rainbow Gathering in Minnesota's Superior National Forest; and at twenty-nine, belly dancing along the Charles River in Cambridge.

"Dance as though no one is watching" became my motto. Stripped of freedom to move in the direction I wanted to, I found a way to feel alive and free. I discovered the truth of Viktor Frankl who wrote in *Man's Search for Meaning*, "When we are no longer able to change a situation, we are challenged to change ourselves." And I'd add "learn to stay present" as we surf the ever-present waves of change.

Change and surf I did. The world opened up a bit at the end of the spring. I found another apartment and moved out. I lived alone, deepened my relationship with myself, and continued to rock dance, which was my Destination Vibration. I became the woman I dreamed of being and was ready to start my new chapter.

It was then that Kenny, carrying two-dozen roses and wheeling a giant cooler filled with basil, squash blossoms, and cauliflower destined for dinner, danced into my life. We met via a dating site called Spiritual Singles. He was "Love Story," and I was "Tiger57."

I'd learned a lot and was now leaning into something very different in terms of relationships. Rather than sparks and lust, I wanted a loving, lasting, soulful connection, combined with shared core values. Today, Kenny and I are writing a love story that we hope will span at least forty-two years. We plan to make it to 100, thanks to our shared interest in and passion for fun and an uber-healthy lifestyle.

While the togetherness is amazing, there is also a shared desire for and support of our individual freedom. I've worked hard to become the jungle tiger I am today, and there is no way I'm going back to the cage-dom I once sought because I was too scared to roam free.

I feel like a kid again. I wake up every morning and have to pinch myself because my life is so rich and beautiful. Never in a million years would I have dreamed up this surf and turf paradise. I thought that I knew what was best for me. I thought I wanted an urban, sophisticated life. The universe knew better. Leaning into the way I wanted to feel—joyful—by visualizing dance brought me to my Destination Vibration.

My wish for you is to discover your Destination Vibration too, and that it will shake you up and energize and empower you to create an amazing next chapter.

In fact, your DV is already created and waiting for you to arrive. You can get there by following any number of different paths. But you have to start. You have to rip the blindfolds off and see things clearly. Only then will you discover that you are exactly where you need to be right now and make the necessary shifts to rock your midlife too.

Start where you are. But please start! We are all in this together. We're no longer old ladies with blue hair, rocking our lives away. We are tens of millions of amazing midlife women changing ourselves and in the process, transforming the face of midlife and the world.

Set an intention to grow and glow because when you shine, you give all of us permission to do the same.

Here is my prayer for you:

May you be happy
May you be healthy
May you live with ease
May you rock your midlife.

PART III

PUTTING IT ALL TOGETHER: ROCK YOUR MIDLIFE IN 7-DAYS

*A journey of a thousand miles begins
with a single step.*

—Confucius

YOUR 7-DAY PLAN FOR ACTION

WELCOME TO *OPERATION: TRANSFORM YOUR LIFE*

Wow! You made it! This is your day. It's time to begin your 7-Day Action Plan. You are at the starting line for Operation: Transform Your Life. No needles or Novocain required, just GRIT (Guts, Resilience, Initiative, and Tenacity) greased with self-love. As your coach and co-pilot, I'm excited that you are here, ready to take action and create a new chapter.

In my work, I meet many amazing, midlife women who want and need to change but are stuck in reverse. They think about change, read about it, dream about it, see other women transform, but never get started. Why? Usually it's one of three things: they are comfortably uncomfortable, afraid—usually of failure, success, or change—or allow their environment to hold them back. Like all of us at midlife, they are running out of time.

As you discovered in Chapter 2: Getting Unstuck, there will always be obstacles keeping you stuck and making change challenging. Here's the thing: the biggest obstacle isn't someone or something standing in your way. The biggest block to your success is between your ears. Your mind, specifically the fearful and self-doubting thoughts, beliefs, and stories you run on repeat, is the only thing holding you back.

That's good news because you can change your thoughts, beliefs, and stories. Doing so will change your life, forever. You can develop the courage to do what scares you and step into the unknown. Each step you take will make you bolder and more accustomed to situations that were once scary. Standing up to your spouse or mother, starting a side hustle, falling in love, speaking in public, going to that exercise class, traveling... Whatever your heart desires, you can have it, but you have to start.

As Eleanor Roosevelt put it: "You gain strength, courage and confidence by every experience in which you really stop to look fear in the face. You are able to say to yourself, *I have lived through this horror. I can take the next thing that comes along.* You must do the thing you think you cannot do."

Before I reveal the detailed plan you can take to jumpstart transforming your life, I want to share one piece of wisdom: Make sure that what *you*—not your spouse, boss, parents, children, or friends—want to change is your own desire. If someone else wants you to change, you may start, but you won't have the hunger and motivation to keep going.

GETTING STARTED

The first thing I want you to do, even before you begin your 7-Day Action Plan, is *write down your goals.* Fact: it's important to vividly write your goals down if you want to achieve them. A study conducted by psychologist Gail Matthews at the Dominican University in California found that you are 42 percent more likely to reach your goals when you write them down. Why? There are two reasons. Writing your goals down and placing them where you will see them daily is a handy visual reminder of what you want to achieve. In addition, when you write something down you increase the chances that you will remember it. Writing enhances *encoding,* a process that takes place in the *hippocampus,* the location in the brain where thoughts are analyzed and either stored in long-term memory or tossed.

So grab your *Rock Your Midlife Playbook*[i] or journal and think about what goals and dreams *you* want to work towards. Write them *all* down. Do you want to know and love yourself more? Have vibrant, radiant health and a clear mind? Fabulous relationships? Do you want to feel empowered and enlightened?

Next, find your *why*, your reasons for changing and moving forward in the direction of your dreams. According to Simon Sinek, author of *Find Your Why* and *Start With Why*, knowing your why—the purpose, cause, or belief that drives you—will guide you toward fulfillment in your personal and professional life. Write down why you want to rock your midlife.

Review what you've written every day. Revise your dreams as you change and grow, and life will show up for you in new, exciting, and unexpected ways. That's called *flow*.

Now take out your calendar and pick a date to start your 7-Day transformation. Make sure to block off at least thirty minutes a day to work on the exercises that follow. You will also need additional blocks of time for some of the activities you will be doing this week, so update your calendar for each new day. It's your life, so please take this seriously and put yourself first. Let the guilt, the shame, the judgment, and all those unproductive emotions and attitudes go. Make this week about *you!*

One final word before we dig in: Don't give up. If you fall down or stumble, make like a toddler learning to walk or a six-year-old learning to ride a bicycle, get back up. Redefine failure. View stumbling blocks as stepping stones on the road towards success. And if you need help and haven't done so already, join my Facebook group, Dr Ellen's Mastermind[v]. It's filled with amazing women who are rocking midlife.

DAY 1: GETTING TO KNOW YOU

Knowing yourself is powerful. Aristotle got it right in his famous dictum, *Knowing yourself is the beginning of all wisdom*. Don't skip this step. It will help you with all the other steps.

To review Step 1, Get To Know Yourself: when you know yourself, you'll be better able to love and validate yourself. You'll be more independent because you won't rely on opinions or positive feedback from others to feel good. Knowing yourself will also provide the clarity to make decisions and put your time and energy into activities that have meaning for you. Finally, it will boost your confidence and help you to connect with your purpose.

Exercise: Discover Your Strengths and Passions

Today's journey begins with a deep journaling exercise to help you discover your strengths and passions. You can't get to know yourself with tons of distraction around you, so find a secluded space where you won't be disturbed. Get still and quiet. Take a few deep, clearing breaths. Let the inhalation nourish you. With each exhalation let go of any ideas around who you're supposed to be.

To start, write down all of your strengths and talents. Don't be humble. Brag as if your life depended on it, which it does. Describe everything that's wonderful and true about you. Write down everything you're good at.

Next, list your passions. Think about what you would do all day if you could or what career you would pick if money weren't an issue. Consider what you loved to do as a child and write it down. This will help you discover more strengths.

Ask a trusted friend, co-worker, or relative to list your strengths. This can be helpful, but listen to what they say with balanced awareness. If something doesn't resonate with you or ring true, let it go.

Take another deep breath and write down your flaws. Suspend judgment. We all have them. It's *common humanity*. Here are some questions to ask yourself: What problems do you have around success and failure? What frustrates you? Where do you slip up? Write these things down. Accept all of yourself.

Action Steps: Once you're done with discovering your strengths, flaws, passions, take the VIA Character Strength Test[ii] if you haven't already done so in Chapter 3. It's free and only takes about ten minutes.

Finally, from all the information you've gathered, select your top three strengths. Find one new way you want to use each of them over the coming week.

DAY 2: BEFRIEND YOURSELF

Today you are going to do two things. First, to inspire and motivate you to take action and get your brain to remember all the reasons to love yourself, I want you to write down your self-love *why*. Then I'm going to provide a powerful exercise that is going to help you express love towards yourself.

As you discovered in Step 2, loving yourself has numerous benefits. You really can't rock your midlife unless you love yourself.

To review, here are some *big* benefits and whys for working on self-love:

• Greater joy, happiness, and wholehearted living
• Better physical and mental health
• More resilience and confidence
• Increased motivation and creativity
• Higher self-esteem and self-worth
• Ability to manifest what you truly want

Grab your *Rock Your Midlife Playbook*[i] or journal and write out your why. If you haven't made your list of the nice things you want to do to love yourself, please do it today. To review Step 2, the five categories in which you can practice self-compassion are body, mind, heart, relationships, and spirit. Keep the list with you so you can refer to it when you need a good friend (you) to provide a pick-me-up.

Exercise: Love Letter to Myself

We often think about telling or showing others how much we love them, but how often do we express love towards ourselves? Think about it: When was the last time you wrote a love letter to yourself and then read it? Never or years ago?

That's about to change because today you are going to take the time to create a handwritten love letter and send it to yourself.

I recommend you use a blank piece of paper or get yourself a beautiful card that resonates with you. Set at least thirty minutes aside to work on this and give yourself permission to enjoy the process. Use colorful markers if you like. Have fun.

Write your letter in the third person as if it's coming from a dear friend. Write it from your heart. For example: Dear (your name), I love you because. I love how you. I'm proud of you because. I love your charming habits, personality quirks, fabulous flaws, etc. You have so many amazing strengths such as. I love your personality. Include a detailed memory or two that makes you smile. Offer some words of comfort for what you might be going through. For example, I know that you are struggling with, and I wanted to let you know that you'll...

Action Step: Seal it up and mail it to yourself. Give yourself a week or two to open it. Set time aside to read and enjoy the beautiful words from you to you.

DAY 3: ENERGIZE YOURSELF

Welcome to Day 3 of your Plan. How did you do with the first two days? How do you feel? I know that working on knowing your strengths and elevating your self-love has energized you. Take a moment to congratulate yourself for completing these actions. Now it's time to work on getting even more energized.

The first thing I would like you to do is commit to one energizing lifestyle change that you do daily and would like to make a long-term habit. This can be big or small. For example, you can choose to drink eight 8-ounce glasses of water, go to bed between 10 and 11 p.m., eat three servings of fruit, or take a thirty-minute daily walk. Write the goal down! When you finish the activity, reward yourself and set an intention to repeat it tomorrow.

Exercise: Your Energy Audit

Today your assignment is to take an inventory of the actions you perform throughout your day. From the moment you wake up to the time you go to sleep, write down the activities you do. As you perform the activity, rate how it makes you feel on a scale of 0 (totally draining) to 10 (fantastic and high vibe). Bonus: You can also take a look at whether or not you are in flow, the state where time seems to sail by because you are so engrossed in what you are doing.

Action Step: Going forward, see if you can do more of the high-energy activities (especially those where you experience flow) on your list that make you feel good and less of the activities that drain you. If you find this helpful, keep track of your energy level for a few more days, including both weekends and weekdays.

DAY 4: REPROGRAMMING *YOUR* MIND

How did you do with your energy audit? I hope that you discovered where some of your energy leaks are and found ways to live a higher-vibe life.

Today we are going to keep the momentum going by helping you to uncover some of your subconscious roadblocks and find ways to relax so you can feel calmer and be clearer.

Revisit the immunity to change information and suggestions in Chapter 2: Getting Unstuck. See if you can identify the competing commitments and big assumptions that are keeping you stuck. How might you test these assumptions so you can move forward? The following exercise will help you to do that.

Exercise: Using The Work

This exercise, called The Work, was created by author and spiritual innovator Byron Katie. Not only will it help you understand subconscious thoughts that drive your behavior and mood, but it will also help you to stop chronic and excessive rumination.

Grab your *Rock Your Midlife Playbook*[i] or journal. Take a few moments to breathe and center yourself. Think about a situation that is bothering you and generating difficult emotions such as sadness, anger, or resentment. Name the emotions (*name it, you tame it)*, then feel the emotion (*feel it, you heal it)*.

Figure out why you are upset (i.e., isolate your stressful thought) and write that down. Take time to journal about the situation so you can discover your true feelings around this issue.

Choose one upsetting thought. Write it down, read it, and ask and journal about the following questions:
1. Is it true?
2. Can I be one-hundred percent sure that it is true?"
3. When I believe this thought, how do I react?
4. Who would I be if I didn't have this belief or thought?

For example, you're upset because you can't seem to stop snacking on junk food at night. Your belief is: I can't stop snacking at night. You ask questions 1 and 2 and realize that you can't be 100 percent sure that the belief is true. When you ask question 3, you realize that you feel bad about yourself and want to snack even more. Then you ask question 4 and realize that if you didn't have that belief, you would feel more capable of making healthier eating choices.

Finally, turn the thought around by listing other thoughts and beliefs that are equally true. For example: *I can stop snacking on junk food at night* or *Other people can stop snacking on junk food at night.*

Action Step: Using any other upsetting thoughts that you are able to identify during the day, challenge your assumptions by putting them through the test of The Work. At the end of the day, write down your new truths!

Finally, today I'd like you to practice doing at least one minute of breathwork. Don't skip this. Breathwork is generally safe and enjoyable, and a great way to reduce stress and increase calm and clarity. Not only is it relaxing and free, but research also shows that it has a positive impact on the heart, brain, and immune and digestive systems.

You can try the practices recommended in Step 4 (box breathing and belly breathing) or try the 4-7-8 method created by Dr. Andrew Weil, M.D. Simply inhale for a count of four, hold it for a count of seven, exhale for a count of eight, and repeat. Notice how it calms down your body and mind, and helps you feel less anxious, angry, or overwhelmed.

DAY 5: EMPOWERING YOU

How are you doing with progressing through the plan? Don't worry if you haven't been able to complete everything in each day's plan. I intentionally made it challenging so you can see how capable you are. Remember, *done* is better than *perfect*. Make any steps forward. Each step forward builds self-confidence, self-esteem, self-love, self-efficacy, and courage.

If you need support at any time in your Rock Your Midlife JOurneY, drop by my private Facebook group, Dr. Ellen's Mastermind[v].

Speaking of courage and encouragement, it's time to build up your empowerment muscle. Please start by grabbing your journal or

Rock Your Midlife Playbook[i], reviewing the definition and examples of what other women have said empowerment means to them in Chapter 7, and then write out what empowerment means to you. Then do the following exercise in which you play with the Law of Attraction to manifest your dreams:

Exercise: Rock Your Midlife Manifestation Mojo

In your *Rock Your Midlife Playbook*[i] or journal, start making your dreams a reality by manifesting what you *really* want by following these steps:

Review the dreams and goals that you wrote down before starting your 7-Day Plan. These dreams are your manifestation foundation. Spend some time looking them over. Ask yourself: Is this what I really want? Get uber specific and clear. For example, if you want a new house, write out all the details: what kind of house, how many rooms, where do you want to live, what type of neighbors and neighborhood do you want, etc.

Write down what it is you want and ask God or the universe for it to manifest, making sure to include the line: *This or something that is better for my highest good.*

1. Visualize all the details as if it's happening using all your senses. Engage with the positive feelings you will experience when you manifest what you want.
2. Create a plan to make it happen. What are the specific action steps you will take to help make it come true?
3. Believe it will really happen. Make sure to address all your limiting beliefs. (Reviewing yesterday's exercise, "The Work," is very helpful here.)
4. Be open to receive. This is where loving yourself and feeling worthy are key.
5. Keep the faith. Manifestation takes time, so trust that

your dream is going to happen, and let go of your timeline and how you think it's supposed to happen.

Action Step: Be intentional by doing at least one of the following practices for today *and* notice how it shifts your vibe:

- Be grateful: Count on all ten fingers something that you are grateful for.
- Write out and repeat an affirmation in the present tense as if it's happening that resonates with you and is about something you want to manifest. For example, *I'm working at the perfect job or my book is a bestseller.*
- Journal about your future when you are living your dream. What does it look and feel like?
- Perform at least one random act of kindness. It helps generate good karma.
- Create a wish list.

DAY 6: REHABBING YOUR RELATIONSHIPS

You are almost done with your 7-Day Plan for Action. Congratulations! Two days to go. How are you feeling? What changes have you noticed in yourself and your life?

As I discussed in Step 6, when you change and transform yourself, not everyone will like the new you and automatically honor your needs. This is why completing the assignments today for creating and enforcing boundaries, practicing saying no, and using Nonviolent Communication are so important.

Remember: Let the guilt go. You're not being selfish. You're practicing self-love by setting boundaries that support and protect you. If setting boundaries is scary, ask yourself: What am I afraid of? Sit with your fear and use The Work from Day 4 of the plan to analyze and challenge your thoughts.

Review the section of Chapter 8, Step 6 on boundaries. Here's a definition that I love from Cheryl Strayed, author of *Tiny Beautiful*

Things, that will inspire and help you: "Boundaries have nothing to do with whether you love someone or not. They are not judgments, punishments, or betrayals. They are a purely peaceable thing: the basic principles you identify for yourself that define the behaviors that you will tolerate from others, as well as the responses you will have to those behaviors."

Exercise: Creating and Enforcing Boundaries

If you haven't done so already, grab your journal or *Rock Your Midlife Playbook* and write out all of your boundaries. Take your time, you can always add boundaries as issues come up. (If you've already done this, turn to the page in your journal and review what you wrote.)

Now you're ready to enforce your boundaries by determining the consequences that will occur when someone crosses the line. This will happen, so decide beforehand what your response will be.

Think about times people have crossed the line and not honored and respected you. In your journal or *Rock Your Midlife Playbook*[i], use the following prompts to help you in the process:

- How would boundaries have improved the situation for you?
- What do you wish you had done or said to protect your possessions, time, energy, and emotional and personal space?
- How could you have been assertive—kind and firm—without being aggressive or angry? What are your roadblocks to establishing and enforcing boundary consequences and how can you leap over them?

Tips for Enforcing Boundaries

Tip #1: When determining consequences, it's helpful to think about these three R's: *related, respectful,* and *reasonable. Related* means the consequences are associated with the violation. For example, if your daughter makes a mess in the kitchen, the consequences are that she has to clean it up. If your husband forgets to do something or show up at the parent-teacher meeting, the consequences could be that you will tell him how you feel. When your friend asks for help *again* but doesn't listen to you, the consequences might be that you stop taking the time to give her advice. *Respectful* means that you don't shame or demean the other person. *Reasonable* means that the consequences aren't outlandish and are something that the other person can do.

Tip #2: Visualization is another effective tool that you can use to set and enforce boundaries. Recall times when someone crossed the line, like when a co-worker asked you to cover a meeting for her or your sister asked you to take care of Mom even though it was her caregiver weekend. See yourself being firm and calling out their BS. You may be feeling uncomfortable as you recall what happened, what was said, and how you'd like to stand up for yourself. That's a good thing. It means you're stepping outside of your comfort zone.

Tip #3: Another way to enforce boundaries is to protect your possessions, space, and time. If you have possessions that you don't want others touching, lock them up. Use passwords on your computer to keep things private. Schedule time for self-care and keep the appointment with yourself. Set auto-responders for emails and the Do Not Disturb feature on your phone for when the workday is done, so you don't have to respond until the next day. Be disciplined about not checking your devices.

Tip #4: If people don't respect your boundaries, they aren't real friends and don't truly care about you. Consider ending the relationship or keeping them at a distance.

Exercise: Practice Saying *No* and Using NVC

Take a deep breath (or review the breathing activity in Day 4) because it's almost time to communicate and share your boundaries, consequences, and needs. Yes, this is hard, which is why you're going to practice right now.

Start by practicing saying *no*. Remember all the times you said yes when you wanted to say no? You can't turn back time, but you can say no now and no the next time and the next. You may feel a little silly. That's okay, but please practice. Here are some sentences to help you:

No, I really can't help you now.

No, I don't have any desire to.

No, I can't or won't do that.

No, I'm not able to do that, but I know someone who may be able to help you.

No, I wish I could, but I'm booked at that time.

Set an intention to say no when you mean no. Know that saying no to someone else is saying yes to yourself.

Finally, I'd like you to practice using Nonviolent Communication (NVC). Think about something that's come up lately with another person that led to a conflict or made you feel bad. Recall what happened and what was said that overstepped your boundaries. Then use the sentence completion below to practice NVC: When _____ (observation) happens, I feel _____.What I need is _____. I'm asking you to _____ (request).

Action Step: Now practice using NVC out loud, preferably with a friend, coach, or therapist with whom you can role-play. Use the example you filled in from the exercise above. How did saying no feel? Don't worry if you don't get it right initially. The fact that you are showing up empowered and communicating *will* shift everything.

Once you've practiced, take your new way of communicating out into the world. You may want to contact the person you had the conflict with from the exercise above and deliver your NVC to them.

DAY 7: ENLIGHTENING YOU

Aaaaaah, you've made it to Day 7. I'm so proud of you and grateful that you are rocking your midlife! Take a moment to appreciate yourself and all you bring to the world.

Today is simple. I'd like you to do two things: First, practice mindfulness (simply being) throughout your day. Second, create a Spiritual Toolkit to support you in your spiritual practice.

I've shared many mindfulness practices in chapters throughout the book because mindfulness is powerful and amplifies every one of the steps. Review how mindfulness can help you to rock your midlife at each step along the way:

- Step #1: You have to observe yourself mindfully to be authentic.
- Step #2: Being mindful is one of the most compassionate, loving things you can do for yourself because it helps to deactivate all the stressful, negative thoughts that keep you sad and stuck.
- Step #3: When you're pooped, notice how you're feeling (being mindful). Taking a couple of mindful breaths and giving yourself what you need to recharge will energize you. Mindfulness also enhances how your body functions so you have more energy.
- Step #4: Mindfulness improves mental health and focus. It clarifies your mind and increases positive feelings.

- Step #5: Mindfulness helps you manage stress and anxiety, and improves resilience and strength, all of which are empowering.
- Step #6: Practicing mindfulness can help shift unconscious behaviors and automatic reactions that have a negative impact on your relationships.
- Step #7: Mindfulness is a very effective spiritual practice. When you engage with the Divine, you experience mindfulness.

While there are many books, websites, and apps to help you practice mindfulness, you actually don't need anything to start. Mindfulness is a gift you can give yourself every moment. What's key is remembering to practice.

Exercise: Practice Mindfulness

In this moment, observe what you are doing. Take one minute to do nothing but focus on your breathing, following each inhalation and exhalation. Describe what you see, hear, smell, taste, and touch. Notice how you are feeling right now.

Set an intention to become more mindful in your life. Make time each day to find mindfulness practices that work for you.

Action Step: Take at least half an hour out of your day to do an activity mindfully that you enjoy, and savor being with yourself

Exercise: Create a Spiritual Toolkit

Wherever you are at on the 7-Steps and in your midlife JOurneY, a Spiritual Toolkit is a welcome companion and a great way to honor and celebrate yourself. It's also great to have around when you experience difficult emotions or have a fight with a loved one or co-worker.

To create your kit, I recommend getting a beautiful box or basket to house all things that inspire, calm, soothe, and center you. You can start by filling it with the list of ways that you'd like to care for yourself and the love letter you wrote to yourself (after it arrives in the mail, of course!) on Day 2. Make sure to place in it *only* things that bring you joy, empower you, and help you connect with your soul.

Here are some suggestions for what to put in your Spiritual Toolkit box:

- Spiritual books and inspiring autobiographies
- Your favorite relaxing, uplifting playlist
- Beads or stones to hold when meditating or praying
- A candle or two to set the mood
- Incense or essential oils to fire up your limbic system, the part of the brain involved in emotional responses
- A healthy, yummy snack
- An adult coloring book (I love mandala books)
- Colored markers, pens, crayons
- Your journal and a pen

Keep your toolkit in a special place and bring it out whenever you feel the need to elevate your consciousness.

A FINAL THOUGHT

Take a breath. Honor yourself. You—yes, *you*—are a miracle. You have everything you need and all the tools to heal and thrive. Now draw on those resources to be, know, love, and empower yourself. Create that great romance, make that career change, go on that trip, write that book, or whatever dream you intend to manifest.

You're a star! Go rock your midlife!

Love and light,
Dr. Ellen, The Midlife Whisperer™

1. 21 THINGS YOU CAN DO TO GET UNSTUCK

When you feel stuck, unmotivated, or in a rut, making a small change or doing something new can help you to move forward. Here's a list of twenty-one things you can do today to create some momentum in your life and get you out of a slump.

1. Declutter

Living in clutter alone can make you feel totally stuck, so take some time to get organized and get rid of anything weighing you down. Start small with a single drawer or closet, or put on some music and hit the garage or an entire floor of your house. This is powerful because it sweeps away the old so you can flow into something new. As you examine your stuff, use this rule: *If you haven't used it, lose it.* Chances are, it's weighing you down and keeping you stuck.

2. Buy a planner

I love gorgeous planners that are chockful of spaces and places to jot down all the things you want to do in your day and week. They usually also come with stickers that you can glue on when you accomplish a task. Full disclosure, I'm super disorganized, so using a planner feels good, and those stickers make me feel like a kid again. Plus, planning how you spend your time and writing down your goals and to-dos is powerful and can get you into action mode.

3. Hydrate

Drinking water throughout your day is an easy habit to make, yet something that is incredibly important. Buy a cute water bottle and set a reminder on your phone, so you'll remember to drink water throughout the day.

4. Sign up for a class

What have you always wanted to learn—photography, growing

flowers, baking cute cupcakes or…? If you can think of it, the class probably exists. After you sign up, put the times you'll be working on the class in your planner.

5. Get an accountability buddy
Find a friend who has a similar goal and work together to accomplish it.

6. Rise with the sun
Try this a couple of times a week and notice how you feel. Even if you are a night owl, being a morning person occasionally will make a huge difference in your motivation and productivity.

7. Play a new song
Do you listen to music throughout the day? Change your playlist. Add more energizing beats and songs that you enjoyed in your youth. You will feel more vibrant and inspired.

8. Create a new habit
Sometimes the easiest way to ditch an old, unwanted habit is to replace it with a new, healthier one. For example, if you're in the habit of having a candy bar in the afternoon, carry a piece of fruit and eat it instead. Tired of biting your nails? Get into the habit of having a weekly manicure. Ruminating when you're anxious or stressed? Get into the habit of doing thirty seconds of deep breathing whenever you notice you're worrying

9. Go somewhere new
When was the last time you took a trip to someplace you've never been? If you can't remember, it's time to go somewhere new. Whether a day trip or a longer vacation, changing your surroundings for hours or days will help you get unstuck and enable you to recharge, so you can see new opportunities.

10. Create a new exercise routine

Moving your body is always a fantastic way to up your energy and get unstuck. To double the effect, try something new that you don't do every day. Take a dance class or a weird form of yoga. kayak, go rock climbing (yes, you can do it!), or swim.

11. Help someone else

Nothing helps you get out of your own way better than helping another person. So volunteer, cook dinner for a neighbor, or call a friend who's been struggling.

12. Get professional help

When all four tires are deep in the mud, it may be time to call a tow truck. This means finding a good therapist or coach who specializes in helping people change their lives. A credentialed, experienced professional can help you look at your beliefs and mindset and help you see what's keeping you in the muck.

13. Change your look

Have a makeover—get a new haircut, change your hair color, or buy new makeup. Buy a new outfit in colors you don't typically wear. You'll feel beautiful and will enjoy the compliments you get.

14. Redecorate

Changing your environment will help you feel like you're living in a new home, so you feel less stuck. Move the furniture around, paint a room, or buy plants, pillows, or pictures.

15. Cook a new recipe

Tired of chicken, chicken, and more chicken? Sick of take-out pizza? Cook something new for dinner. Most people have a dozen or so recipes that they rotate. There are millions of recipes online to try.

What foods do you love or what have you always wanted to make? Tiramisu, chia pudding, bread, Pad Thai? Go for it.

16. Check out a biography
Whether you read it, listen to it, or watch the movie version, find an inspiring woman and check out her story. Here are some suggestions: Helen Keller, Frieda Kahlo, Indira Gandhi, Charlotte Bronte, Marie Curie, Michelle Obama, Flo Kennedy, Wangari Maathai, Malala Yousafzai, Eleanor Roosevelt, Cleopatra, Catherine the Great, and Maya Angelou.

17. Visualize
Visualization is powerful and helps to change the structure of your brain so you feel more confident and motivated. Here's a simple visualization exercise that can help you get unstuck. Close your eyes and take a few deep breaths. Now using all your senses, imagine your inner strength. What pictures come to mind? What does your inner strength look, feel, sound, smell, and taste like? Write the results down in your journal and bring this image to mind when you need a boost to get moving.

18. Set an intention to embrace the new
Intention setting—writing down what you intend to do—will help you to embrace something new. You can make it specific, as in "I intend to start/stop/change(fill in the blank)," or more general, as in "I intend to be open to new people, places, and things."

19. Review your strengths
Review Chapter 3, Step 1, and if you haven't done so already, discover your strengths. Write them down. Keep the list in your wallet, and take it out when your confidence is low and you're feeling stuck.

20. *Meditate*

Even a couple of minutes a day will help you observe rather than react to the thoughts and beliefs that are keeping you stuck.

21. *Commit to a 30-Day Challenge*

These are always fun, inspirational, and motivational. There's something about the camaraderie you feel that keeps you going. Follow me on social media to learn when my next 30-day challenge is.

BONUS: build positive energy, see how blessed you are, and realize how much is right with you and your life.

2. RESOURCES

Books

Brown, Brené. *The Gifts of Imperfection: Let Go of Who You Think You're Supposed to Be and Embrace Who You Are.* New York: Hazelden Publishing, 2010.

Burnett, Bill and Evans, Dave. *Designing Your Life: How to Build a Well-Lived, Joyful Life.* New York: Knopf, 2016.

Cuddy, Amy. *Presence: Bringing Your Boldest Self to Your Biggest Challenges.* New York: Little Brown, Spark, 2015.

Dispenza, Joe. *Breaking the Habit of Being Yourself: How to Lose Your Mind and Create a New One.* Carlsbad: Hay House Publishing, 2013.

Fredrickson, Barbara. *Positivity: Groundbreaking Research to Release Your Inner Optimist and Thrive.* New York: One World, 2011.

Germer, Chris. *The Mindful Path to Self-Compassion: Freeing Yourself From Destructive Thoughts and Emotions.* New York: Guilford Press, 2009.

Hanson, Rick. *Buddha's Brain: The Practical Neuroscience of Happiness, Love, & Wisdom.* Oakland: New Harbinger Publications, 2009.

Kabat-Zinn, Jon. *Full Catastrophe Living: Using the Wisdom of Your Body and Mind to Face Stress, Pain, and Illness.* New York: Random House, 1990.

Kegan, Robert and Laskow Lakey, Lisa. *Immunity to change: How to Overcome It and Unlock the Potential in Yourself and Your Organization.* Boston: Harvard Business School Press, 2009.

Loehr, Jim and Schwartz, Tony. *The Power of Full Engagement: Managing Energy, Not Time, Is the Key to High Performance and Personal Renewal.* New York: Free Press, 2003.

Neff, Kristin and Germer, Christopher. *The Mindful Self-Compassion*

Workbook: A Proven Way to Accept Yourself, Build Inner Strength, and Thrive. New York: Guilford Press, 2018.

Robbins, Mel: *The 5 Second Rule: Transform Your Life, Work, and Confidence with Everyday Courage. New York:* Savio Republic, 2017.

Rosenberg, Marshall B. *Nonviolent Communication: A Language of Life.* Encinitas: PuddleDancer Press: 2015.

Seligman, Martin, E.P. *Authentic Happiness: Using the New Positive Psychology to Realize Your Potential for Lasting Fulfillment.* New York: Simon and Schuster, 2002.

Websites

Dr. Ellen Albertson, RD, PhD: http://www.drellenalbertson.com

The Center for Mindful Self-compassion: https://centerformsc.org/

Dr. Kristin Neff: https://www.self-compassion.org

UMass Memorial Health Center for Mindfulness: https://www.ummhealth.org/center-mindfulness

The Five Tibetan Rites: https://www.youtube.com/watch?v=j_bY6REpIPE

Endnotes

[1] Rock Your Midlife Playbook: http://eepurl.com/hLIK7n

[2] The VIA Institute Character Strengths Test: https://www.viacharacter.org

[3] The Wingfinder by Red Bull: https://www.redbull.com/int-en/wingfinder

[4] The High 5 Test: https://high5test.com

[5] Dr Ellen's Mastermind: https://www.facebook.com/groups/drellensmastermind

[6] Raise Your Vibe Quiz: https://raiseyourvibequiz.com

ACKNOWLEDGEMENTS

It takes a village to birth a book, and I am grateful for so many people who have supported me during the writing, editing, and publishing process.

First, I have to thank all of my amazing clients. Working with each of you has inspired me and made it possible for me to develop the 7 Steps to transform detailed in this book. Thank you for trusting me and having the courage to transform. I'm grateful for all the amazing fans, friends, and followers that I get to interact with every day on social media. All of you help motivate me and I'm grateful for the support you give me. When you shine you give all women permission to do the same.

With great gratitude I want to thank my incredible man, Kenny who challenges me to reach higher, have more fun, and of course eat more kale. You make everyday a wonderful midlife adventure. Thanks for believing in me and helping me edit the book. I am also grateful for my Dad who has supported me throughout my entire life and been an amazing example of how to live courageously with meaning and purpose.

I want to thank my editor and coach, Nancy Marriot for believing in me and this project, encouraging and nurturing me as a writer, and helping me make this book a reality. Nancy, you truly were my book midwife. I'd also like to thank book and writing coach, Paula Diaco who helped me with the early stages of outlining the book. I also must thank my patient book designer, Lucy Holtsnider for gracefully supporting me through the book production process.

I must acknowledge Margaret Moore and Wellcoaches for helping me develop stellar coaching skills along with all the incredible teachers who shared their techniques for helping people thrive. A special thank you to Kristin Neff and Christopher Germer, who created the Mindful Self-compassion program that transformed me and is one of the focal points of this book. Additionally, thank you Kristin for your mentorship and support during my self-compassion research.

A final shout-out to the amazing team at Self Publishing School (SPS), my SPS coach Brett Hilker, and all the incredible writers who are students at SPS. I've learned so much from all of you and appreciate your ongoing support.

ABOUT THE AUTHOR

Dr. Ellen is a Psychologist, Registered Dietitian, Board Certified Health and Wellness Coach, Reiki Master, and Mindful Self-compassion Teacher. Known as The Midlife Whisperer™, she helps women raise their vibration so they have the energy, confidence, and clarity to make their next chapter their best chapter.

An author, inspirational speaker and expert on women's wellbeing, Dr. Ellen has appeared on *Extra*, the Food Network and *NBC World News* and has been quoted in *Psychology Today*, *Eating Well*, and *USA Today*. She has written five books and articles for *SELF*, *Better Homes & Gardens* and *Good Housekeeping*.

She brings over 25 years of counseling, coaching, and healing experience to her holistic practice and transformational work. She lives on the Champlain Islands of Vermont with her high-tech, raw-food loving partner, Ken and her tree climbing Border Collie, Rosie.

You can connect with her on...
Instagram: https://www.instagram.com/the_midlife_whisperer/
Facebook: https://www.facebook.com/groups/drellensmastermind
Twitter: https://twitter.com/rockyourmidlife
Linkedin: https://www.linkedin.com/in/drellenalbertson/
DrEllenAlbertson.com

CAN YOU HELP?

THANK YOU FOR READING MY BOOK!

I love hearing what readers have to say and would appreciate receiving your feedback.
I need your input to make the next version of this book—and my future books—better.
Please leave me an honest review on Amazon, letting me know what you thought of the book.

Thanks so much!

Printed in Great Britain
by Amazon

74952638R00147